THE WAY OF DEMONS

The Way of Demons © 2020 Simon Bastian
All Rights Reserved World wide.
Front cover (pb), back cover (hb) image: detail from *Zhong Kui going on an Excursion* by
Gong Kai (1222-1307).
Bamboo Slips of the Chiah text, p. 46, Harvard-Yenching Institute.
Graffiti, Granada, 2017, p. 47, © Simon Bastian.
Demon Mask, p. 84, The Canadian Society for Asian Arts.
Hand Forms, pp. 135-140, © Simon Bastian. With thanks to Bethan for the
photography.
Gratitude also to *History of Masks*.

ISBN 978-1-907881-91-6 (Hardcover)
ISBN 978-1-907881-92-3 (Paperback)

First published in 2020 by Hadean Press
www.hadeanpress.com
Keighley, West Yorkshire
England

THE WAY OF DEMONS

Shadow and Opposition in
Taoist Thought, Ritual and Alchemy

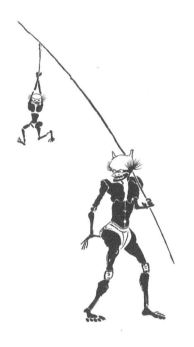

SIMON BASTIAN

With love to Lynn

ACKNOWLEDGEMENTS

Thanks to Lynn as ever for her support and encouragement during this project.

Much gratitude to Erzebet for incisive editing and for the production.

I was very fortunate in having found a teacher during the 1990s who instructed me in the Yuan Qi Internal Alchemy Qi Gong from Chen Yan Feng via Mt. Emei: Master John Barber.

And finally, love to all my family.

S.B. 2020

Contents

Introduction: Defining Tao

Because of the general ambiguity in interpreting the terms 'Tao' and 'Taoism', it is important to specify in what sense they are being used, whether as philosophy, religion, as informing social conduct, or as a matter of personal ideology. This is still a matter of warm if not heated debate amongst academics, so it can be even more of a problem for the interested lay reader. There are now online courses on 'How to Become a Taoist Master/Sage/Monk', even offering certificated Priest training. The New Age has produced its own form of Tao, where it is all things to all people.

In the past as a matter of convenience definition has been divided between 'Tao chia' and 'Tao chiao', respectively schools of philosophy and religion, but there again the 'orthodox' religious Taoism may subsume magical practices. ('Isms' can be divisive, and particularly 'Taoism' seems an awkward term, but of necessity we will continue its use.) A Taoist might be a mystic, priest, monk, lay member of a sect, healer, shaman, occultist, seeker of immortality or anti-social nonconformist. Although Taoism may have an image of isolated hermits retreating to the mountains, an essential duty is social service, vital for those following the path of spiritual immortality. The Taoist masters did not set themselves apart from society. As the Tao is universal, it is not in itself sectarian, and is not defined as belonging to a specific section of the population or a class division.

The very nature of being indistinct, vague and amorphous is one identification of the Tao. This is misleading, and due to incomplete translations of the *Tao Te Ching* as a scripture, when it does not have the same liturgical status as other religions' Holy Books. In trying to form set definitions we might refer to Deleuze and Derrida who suggest that everything is in a state of becoming rather than being static, or to F. C. Happold, who calls Tao '...the Primal Meaning and Undivided Unity behind everything', out of which came polar opposites, conditioning our perception of the universe, a 'dilemma of duality'.

As either comparative religion or philosophical system, it is perhaps simplistic to see the two great Chinese traditions as being antithetical: as examples of, on the one hand, bureaucracy and convention – the Orthodox conservative Confucian values, versus the counter-cultural, anti-hierarchical rebellious heterodoxy of Taoism on the other. As Joseph Needham put it in *Science and Civilization in China* (1956), 'Taoism was religious and poetical, yes; but it was also at least as strongly magical, scientific, democratic, and politically revolutionary'. Within the perception of Taoism as *informal* lies a rigorous formal structure.

Confucian and Taoist ideologies could also be seen as constituting a complementarity as a Yin-Yang duality. They were not necessarily antagonistic at all levels of culture, politics, and social class. Confucianism would be classed as Yang authoritarianism, with Taoism adopting the Yin position of opposition in the shadows. State Confucianism was a contamination of the real teachings, suppressing women and free thought and concentrating power in the hands of men with a system of social hierarchy. Taoism gives prominence to the Feminine, both in principle of equality and in practice in its admittance of women on a complete parity. Any deviation from this (and there can be in some sects) is, it might be said, not truly the Tao. There may seem to be a contradiction in how the 'Te' in *Tao Te Ching* is usually interpreted as Power or Virtue, if considering the root of the word as coming from the Latin *Virtus* and *Vir*, a masculine connotation, whereas the Tao's creative Power is effectively and most particularly 'Feminine'. But the philosophy isn't dependent upon simplistic typing.

The idea of a global synthesis of belief systems met through the Information revolution, a cultural fusion, is opposed by a counter-reaction of aggressive re-emergent nationalism and the demonising of not only sub-cultures but also of any classification of people accorded perceived difference. Difference as Identity means reaction, but the contrast in duality is all too often unfortunately seen as a negative factor, only to be resolved in antipathetic ways. The Taoist term *wu-ji-bi-fan* is relevant here: things reverse upon reaching an extreme. In the West this might be complemented by the term *enantiodromia*: finding an equilibrium where extremes are opposed. That which defies 'The Common Good' is turned into a Demon, a Shadow. A shadow is cast as a dark double of something or someone, not a completely alien object but part of the whole. Recognition rather than rejection of this is integral to the Taoist construct of Yin-Yang dualism, where every particle and event merges into a flowing continuum.

What is presented here then, in the spirit of this definition, is the Yin aspect of Taoist practice and theory, which can be called its Shadow side. Demons as a term or categorization will be examined through the common if not exhaustive range of societal, psychological and supernatural interpretation, and via the prism of what is called Western Taoism (due to its approach from location, background and understanding being set apart from the Chinese cultural version). To a Western Taoist particularly at this unpleasant time of extremism in political direction, the world of demons is an inventive and challenging resource.

Kleeman ('Daoism in the Third Century', in *Purposes, Means and Convictions in Daoism*, p. 12) notes claims by early external accounts, not documented in surviving scriptures, that followers of the faith were referred to as 'demon troopers' (*guizu*), and the religion could be defined as a 'demonic way' (*guidao*). Far from having a negative connotation, this is as much a part of The Way as its shadowless Yang counterpart. Its answers to explicit opposition are indispensable for a Western cultural integration. In fact, being bound to earth and subject to all grades of demonic forces as we humans are, it is a vital study.

NOTE

As in my previous books, I have tended to use what system of transliteration has seemed most familiar or appropriate for any particular term, so I am not consistent in my use of either the Wade-Giles or Pinyin. For example, generally most people are now familiar with the name 'Beijing' in place of 'Peking', but 'Tai Chi' is still more accepted than 'Taiji'. If I occasionally veer towards the idiosyncratic in my selection of translation, I apologise. Inexactitude is a continuous hazard encountered in East-West dialogue, and cultural context may be necessarily considered. Besides, Thomas Francis Wade and Herbert Giles detested each other, and it seems a shame to consign to extinction a system built in an atmosphere of mutual loathing.

The Chinese language as magical resource is apparent in its pictograms, which in themselves can be used as meditative sigils and talismans, some of which derive from oracular scripts such as the Bone Oracle. For the Western practitioner, the ideograms being far removed from the usual concept of an alphabet lends a further dissociative effect.

I am making a differentiation between *The Way of Demons* as a title to indicate an exploration of the Yin symbolic sphere of influence and counterpoint in Taoism, and conducting an exercise in comparativism if not even synthesis, and Yao Tao, the Way of the Demon, which is a term for sorcery with a negative connotation.

Tao is incidentally pronounced Dao (*dow*), as it is most often now spelt. My reason for retaining the T will be made clear in due course.

Radical 194: Demon or Ghost

Oracle Bone Script

Seal Script (common through the latter half of the 1st Millennium BCE)

The Kangxi radical (the radicals are graphical components of Chinese characters) for demon or ghost can be traced to the Oracle Bone script dating from the late 2nd Millennium BCE carved onto animal bones or turtle shells and used in divination.

APPROPRIATE APPROPRIATION

'Cultural renewal comes about when highly differentiated
cultures mix.' Alan Watts.

THE POSITIONING, or bluntly appropriating, of Taoist studies into a
European thought frame didn't raise any question of correctness, in
the nervous modern sense, for those 19th to early 20th century French
esotericists who brought Taoist texts under the ambit of the perennial
teaching, and tangentially supplemented the research by scholars
such as the 'School of Paris' led by Maspero. Esoteric Taoism forms
its own historical thread, with Liebniz around two hundred years
earlier likening Chinese ideograms to his idea of a universal language
or *characteristica universalis*, and perhaps being influenced by Taoist
thought in his concept of the Monadology.

Comparisons between Taoism and other religions found favour
as aspects of the 'perennial wisdom'. John-Gustaf Agueli was a
member of the Paris Theosophical Society and an initiate of a Sufi
order. He wrote an article on the similarity between Tao and Islam for
La Gnose, Rene Guenon's periodical (1907). His knowledge of Taoism
came from Albert Puyon, Comte de Pouvourville, who it seems was
initiated into a Chinese secret society that year. And as a third note for
1907, Puyon co-authored *Les Enseignments Secrets de le Gnose*, referred to
by Guenon as making a connection between Taoism and Gnosticism.
Another member of both a Sufi order and the (in this case American)
Theosophical Society was C.H. Bjerregaard, who gave a series of
lectures on The Inner Life and the *Tao-The-King* (sic) in 1912. Guenon
wrote *Apercus sur l'Esoterisme Islamique et le Taoisme* along with several
other books using Taoist ideas, and more recent contributors to the
presentation of parallels between the Tao and Sufism/Islam have
included the Japanese writers Toshihiko Izutsu and Sachiko Murata.
Taoism and Kabbalah have similarly been compared, from Martin
Buber to Eric Yudelove and others.

There is admittedly a confirmation bias in our reading of
translated texts being moulded by our own values and perceptions. It

is superficial to try reading the minds of ancient Chinese philosophers from the perspective of an information-society present moment. It's a hard enough act of the imagination attempting to inhabit the consciousness of an Iron Age Celt, let alone that of a Warring States bureaucrat.

Our cultural history is shaped from the Enlightenment value of The Individual, and the outcome at this particular time is prominently described as 'Relative Truth'. By this measurement, the Tao is either appropriated as some universal commodity, disregarding its cultural, historical and geographical foundation, or condemned to isolation from the masses. Chinese thought, and by extension Taoist thought, does inescapably proceed in a different manner than we may be accustomed to. For a start, the written language, with its elegant ideograms composed by pictorial elements, is far more exotic than our meagre alphabet. And the Chinese view of the world, socially, collectively and through ideas of the self, is doubtless contrary to that of the West as has been acknowledged by Chinese sociologists (see Yang and Gao, 1991).

On its own terms, elements have been and are selectively adopted, such as the European-American model of psychology and therapy, including the Cognitive Behavioural. The psychiatrists Yalin Zhang and Dersen Young developed Chinese Taoist Cognitive Psychotherapy (CTCP) in 1992, using Taoist principles combined with the Cog. B. form of mental health treatment, because they recognised that Chinese attitudes and ingrained forms of thought needed adapted techniques applied. Simply using the Western model without culturally sympathetic adaptation would not work.

Popular modern interpretations of Taoism, including the *Tao of Pooh* (quite obviously never intended seriously) tend to fare badly under the scrutiny of sinologists. Ursula K. Le Guin's *Lao Tzu Tao Te Ching* particularly was criticised as an example of all that is wrong in populist adaptations of the Tao. Though Jonathan R. Herman in his 1998 review said it was 'an intelligent example of the emerging Western transformation of Taoism', Russell Kirkland called it a 'narcissistic pseudo-translation'. But really, all Le Guin did was make 'a rendition, not a translation' as she put it herself, so to view it as a perverse divergence from scholastic contributions is setting a highly selective parameter for the subject.

In fact the *Tao Te Ching* was reworked and reinterpreted from a very early stage. If we acknowledge the Taoist tradition as it was led by a social and political elite and keep in mind how we personally approach it, there is surely still room for re-interpretation and adaptation to an occidental sensibility. In any case we could regard the Tao as anti-intellectual; in Chapter 18 Lao-tzu says, 'When intellectuals arose, great artifices began'.

With regard to the 'Cultural Appropriation' by students interpreting Taoist practices or even (necessarily) modifying them (Kirkland referred to the West's interpretation of Taoism as 'cultural theft' and 'spiritual colonialism'), we could note that while history is based on appropriation, so is progress.

Western Taoism is a term treated with some suspicion, a fear of the source's degradation, and writing under the idiom is a difficult combination of juggling act and tightrope walk. Between the austere demands of the academics and the depredations of Aquarian Age One Religion proponents it is rare to find no one taking exception to the balancing required. Ideally, there is something to be gained from every new exploration of the Path. Like Le Guin's take on Lao Tzu, it may not meet with approval by the conservative scholastic set, but it can offer new insights, or variations on themes. In this Way, the Tao is multifaceted, reflecting different views regardless of national background.

Assimilation and the transference of art and knowledge cross-culturally is, it might be judged, a token of respect. Even faced with the charge of heresy, Islamic and Oriental arts and sciences seeped undeterred into the fabric of the West. (Gordan Djurdjevic suggests 'esotericism' as 'a more appropriate correlate' than the word heresy which has cultural limitation.) Ceremonial magicians, Neoplatonists and alchemists during the Middle Ages were instrumental in marrying new thought and artistic expression through cultural fusion. But of course we also need to pay attention to traditional representation in the course of adapting, and not fall prey to subjective wish fulfilment and selectivity. Myth, as illustration, has great power in it, but when it is subverted to suit a need to devalue it into something less threatening and more *acceptable*, or depotentised, then its validity is tarnished.

Really, returning to our specific subject, all that is required is the honesty to say what is a Western version of Taoism and what is the original material. The West's version is young and in the process of taking form; that does not invalidate it from having efficacy. The Tao is global. How we tap into it independently of national boundaries is the current question. If it was insisted upon, I would be perfectly happy to reframe my use of the term 'Taoism' as 'Dialectical Monism'. What's in a name? As the tradition of mysticism would put it, the whole is a duality, a unity of polarities.

THE MAGICAL WORLD

Black and White Ouroborous: the words are 'The All is One'.
From the work of Cleopatra the Alchemist, Egypt c. 3rd Century.

The distinction of Taoist Magic from other forms is necessarily its foundation in Tao as an operative sphere and as the source of the practitioner's intuition and power. The magician as a moral being in an amoral universe creates a structural tension that is a component in resolution toward desired end results.

Resource to true Chinese magical tradition is limited by admission, requiring for one thing a fluency in a relevant language, be it Mandarin, Cantonese or a variant, or a South East Asian language, as well as a lengthy judgement of character by the heads of whatever lineage one wishes to enter. The traditions are now usually found in Taiwan, Malaysia, Indonesia and Thailand due to the Cultural Revolution and previous centuries of a gradual eradication of the temples having alienated practitioners of these arts. Also there is misleading representation by so-called 'Taoist sorcerers' charging heavy fees.

What is more accessible to the student in the West however are the methods of Taoist Inner Alchemy from a competent Qi Gong master. With practice, these can lead in the same direction as sorcery. A practical outline of this methodology will be presented in later chapters.

One of the Gnostic heresies was that 'human beings make gods, and worship their creation' (Gospel of Philip) – that Anthropos or humanity was the primal creator. Throughout history and culture the godlike character varies. We could say gods are 'first things', originators, prime movers. They envelop us, are the source of some ultimate truth and power, or are adopted as templates for identity, the Magus becoming god-like in his control of nature, the Warrior in his power over life and death. Myth and magic originate in the personification of phenomena by personal consciousness, every object or force being given animation. Gods are created in our likeness, rather than the appropriated reverse.

There are gods now in the process of being created by us. These may take the form of Artificial Intelligence, or be purely of our own imagination, because practically everything that we are and own came from our own thoughts and visions. Our projections are too often of abominations, turning the daimonic into the demonic. It is the sense of challenge that informs our creation, a need for struggle. Making the quest for new knowledge a dangerous and fraught one is the only way we know to make it worthwhile. If we don't battle monsters, how can we be heroic? It is simply a problem of perspective; inadvertently is created evil.

The fundamental instincts are fear and love, or death and sex. In the face of the unknown, the reaction is to worship the awe-inspiring as the apotheosis of one or the other of these instincts. With night and darkness associated with sleep/death, the dawn indicated a rebirth, a return to life. The Return became a foundation for religious belief. Duality also emerged, from the observation of shadows, echoes and reflections as a double existence, a world shadowing the physical, and so images, copies in the form of idols, statues and icons, were used as a focus for projection.

As language and script developed, alongside mathematics and geometry, abstract symbols could become imbued with power, leading to the formation of talismans and diagrams as representing the 'ground plan' of the universe, or the Thought within God's Mind as Emanation. Jacques Lacan argued that the unconscious is structured like a language, recalling Heidegger's dictum that language is the 'house of being'.

Animals, plants, and stones became worshipped or revered not for their own qualities as much as for being representative of a being, or an image of a characteristic. An idol became the actual abode of a god through consecration. Personification in itself was not religion, although it laid the ground for such. Behind monotheism and polytheism lay the impersonal force of creation. Elemental forces such as fire, wind, and thunder became gods, the sun, moon and stars too. Every force of nature became a deity through animism, the attributing of a conscious power. Although gods are certainly not by any means paragons of virtue (look at the Greek pantheon), due to the essential dual nature of human consciousness with its bi-hemispheric brain, the demonic arose.

How the Tao is concerned with demons is in the classification of these entities and their actions into negative or positive, as in the philosophical concept of Yin and Yang. Because a Taoist view of the spirit world is its emanation through the physical body, we can see demons in a psychological form of complex which is as valid as are independent entities. Through divination systems and ritual we can communicate with this side of life in order to achieve a synthesis – the work of Alchemy as Jung would recognise it – and we can identify anomalies in our environment as demonic, i.e. disruptive influences.

The magical world summons a feeling, a sense of presence. We can add the word 'divine' to amplify this sensation, defined by William James as not only 'the primal and enveloping and real' but also that which is responded to with a solemnity and gravity. In the translating of mystical experience by writing about it we have to fall back on sensory analogue: touch, or a physical function such as 'the Breath of God'. As Kant expressed it, although our concepts of God or the design of the universe are not properly objects of knowledge, being objects without a sense-content, we can act as if they are real. We make real our perceptions through the human quality of abstraction, a feeling for reality that goes beyond sense-content. The sense of reality has its counterpart in a sense of unreality, and the entirety of our mental life would be severely curtailed if we only insisted upon a rationalist assessment of its observations.

Magical Reality, the world of our imagining which may by a subtle process be translated into real world effect, is unique for each of us, so we set forth (or are cast adrift) in our own inner space, which can be daunting. That is why pioneers in the alternate philosophy formed guiding imagery along the way, such as the idealisation of the 'Spiritual Warrior', or the Grail Knight, which has been formulated over centuries. The qualities of the warrior – strength, courage, steadfastness – were invoked as essentials for inner journeys.

The Gnostic recommendation of self-knowledge, psychology as religion, expressed by Valentinus in terms of the four elements is much the same path utilised today. An addition of 'Spirit' produces diagrammatically the Pentagram, the five-pointed star. Integrating the elements is a well-recognised means of balancing the psyche, as used both in Western initiatory esotericism and Taoist Inner Alchemy. Having a keen awareness of reality is vital for involvement in both magical and martial practice, otherwise we may delude ourselves as to the effectiveness of what we actually do. Therefore the emphasis on achieving psychological balance is an essential foundation for either study, symbolized as Inner Alchemy.

To remain unconscious is resistance to gnosis. It is stated that enlightened consciousness, the 'Kingdom', is not to be expected as an historical event: 'When you make the two one, and when you make the inside like the outside and the outside like the inside, and the above like the below, and when you make the male and the female one and the same…Then you will enter [the Kingdom]' (Gospel of Thomas). Essentially the Yin-Yang doctrine of Tao.

Foreign Devils: Tao in the West

'There could be shadow galaxies, shadow stars, and even shadow people.' Stephen Hawking.

In Tanizaki's *In Praise of Shadows*, light and dark are used to compare the cultural contrast between the West and East, with the East appreciating the subtlety of shadow whereas the West only looks for light, and everything has to be apparent.

The use of the term *gui* (*devil*, in this sense) in relation to foreigners goes back to the 16th and early 17th centuries (Ming dynasty, 1368-1644) when the Portuguese and Dutch arrived. By the mid-19th century it was used for missionaries whose Christianity was associated with imperialism. In contrast, in the Taiping movement (1851-64), the leader Hong Xiuquan believed it was his mission to get rid of demons in China, by which he meant the followers and administrators of orthodox Confucianism and Qing officials. Demonisation was applied not only to the foreign, but to groups within Chinese society; demon as a label became a means of Othering. *Yang guizi*, 'foreign devils/demons', was applied to Westerners, 'The West' being inclusive of both Europe and North America. The Human was equated with the Chinese themselves, with demons being outside that realm. The Foreign/Western was by implication demonic.

In a way it does not necessarily denote being evil as such; *gui* were interpreted as being outsiders and strangers. It was also not purely a matter of the West being vilified, as long before the Ming Dynasty ethnic groups in China dehumanised each other and minorities were alienated. The author Jin Yong's self-castrated gay character Dongfang Bubai is indirectly described with the Chinese word *yao*, *demon* or *monster*, the intention being to reflect the prevailing attitude towards anything other than heterosexual relations. In the People's Republic, homosexuality was banned until its legalization in 1997, and was only declassified as a mental illness in 2001.

Other than other is a marginalising category. In Chinese translation, *Chule qita*, that which is 'Other than other', may register as alien, or indeed demonic.

Apart from the considerable work undertaken in establishing Esoteric Taoism toward the latter part of the 19th century, most European sinologists took their impression of Taoism from Confucian interpreters who were naturally biased. This resulted in the major part of it being dismissed as superstition, as the religious and philosophical aspects were divided.

Outside of China we are more familiar with Taoist philosophy, as exemplified by the *Lao-tzu* and the *Chuang-tzu*, known as the 'Lao-Chuang'. These two most commonly referred to texts are not by any means the totality of what Taoism comprises. (Taoism is also sometimes called Huang-Lao Teaching, after the Emperor Huang-Ti and Lao-tzu). The earliest translation of the *Tao Te Ching* was a Latin version presented to the British Royal Society in 1788 produced by Jesuit missionaries, while John Chalmers made the first English translation in 1868.

Although the 1970s in Britain was a decade of dystopia, with its strikes, power cuts and casual violence, the time was ready for a new sense of global integration and communication. It was just at the point when the planet's external reach was diminishing, with the American space missions beginning to find their economic limitations.

Nixon had made the trip to China in 1972, bridging the political gulf between East and West, but the individual who truly represented the new *entente* was Bruce Lee. As a Chinese-American, he even physically embodied the new era of openness. Martial arts, 'Kung Fu', became the medium for a popular translation of Chinese culture into Western consciousness, reaching beyond its physical boundaries. Lee died at 32, a charismatic-tragic figurehead for a modern multiculturalism.

A whole industry emerged, and Chinese classics were transferred into pop culture including *The Water Margin* and *Monkey*. The TV show *Kung Fu* had scenes of borderline magic, with the lead character Caine walking on rice paper in the opening credits without leaving a trace. European esoteric ideas began to be processed into and through Taoist esotericism, with Western students of Chinese teachers influencing in turn Chinese/Asian teachers such as Hua Jing Ni and Mantak Chia to produce syncretic applications.

Escape and Power were the themes that dominated at a time when *Clockwork Orange* was banned as being too close to reality for comfort. Tao was an answer for those seeking some spiritual path not provided by monolithic, monotheistic state-sponsored religion.

THE WEST'S ENGAGEMENT WITH DUALITY

Bemused curiosity rather than connectivity is probably the general public attitude, but Taoism has permeated into Western consciousness through symbolism such as the *taijitu* or Yin-Yang symbol, a ubiquitous feature of car bumper stickers and badges throughout the 1960s alongside the CND emblem. In its physical expression, the art of Tai Chi Chuan gained popularity when Chinese teachers fled the Cultural Revolution and began classes in free-thinking California.

To make a comparison with another classical form of philosophy, Stoicism's view of living in accordance with a supreme principle or power, of finding a natural path, bears much of a resemblance to Taoism, as does its goal of striving toward *arete*, rendered as virtue (*Te*). Seneca may be compared to Chuang-tzu in humanizing the teaching, as the severe sages of either school of thought could seem far removed from the concerns of daily living. Rather than exalting a god or gods, to the Stoics the human was paramount. Similarly, to Taoists gods and other beings are mythic/symbolic forces with no particular religious connotation, being representative of states or qualities within oneself. As internal images, they are aids to self-cultivation. Seneca also advanced the idea that all are equal regardless of 'station' in life.

It was of course Carl Gustav Jung who saw Eastern and especially Taoist principles in light of a modern psychological reading, with his analysis of alchemical texts such as *The Secret of the Golden Flower* (*T'ai I Chin Hua Tsung Chih*) as a way toward integrating dark and light in the psyche.

Dualism is an unavoidable feature in the West's excursions into philosophy, psychology and physics; the Mind-Body problem and the categorical separation of reality into the material and immaterial creates a metaphysical dualism inclusive of Good and Evil as profound opposites. A state of duality pervades all aspects of life, whether harmoniously or antagonistically: *chiaroscuro* in art, counterpoint in music; in politics, Left and Right, socialist and capitalist.

Binary opposition as a linguistic concept comes from structuralist theory and Saussure, and binomial conditions are outlined throughout our customs and pastimes from the old marriage vows of 'For richer, for poorer, In sickness and in health' to sport and competitions. The West has further divided itself from The East into The Old World and The New World: Europe and America. There are also the sociological class divisions, rich and poor, one community or culture often at variance with another: Us and Them.

The antipathy between art and science, the Two Cultures debate, and identity issues involving terms such as gender neutrality and non-binary are other areas of contention seeking resolution within an apparent inexorable duality. It is a natural universal conclusion in our experience of the world and the phenomena we are subject to. Epistemological dualism of subject and object differs from a straight comparison with Yin-Yang theory due to the latter tending to favour an implied eventual merging of contrasting forces.

Illustration from 'The Dragon, Image and Demon', 1887.

As a Taoist saying goes, *The World is Opposition*. The trouble has been in finding a unification. The Paradoxical is also a core device in the Taoist panoply of thought tech, in a similar vein to Chan

Buddhism, which developed in the 6th Century CE, and became Zen. *Insolubilia* forms an integral part of philosophical investigation, such as the opposition between unity and plurality. Paradox, contrast, oxymorons, antithesis and antonyms, juxtaposition: the variety of linguistic, semantic conundrums that form a thread in postmodernist cogitation are a parallel to a Taoist line of thought. Likewise, the counter-intuitive, along with the Counter-Culture, echo a rebelliousness found in Chuang-tzu, of going against the grain, of boats against the current.

'Opposition thinking' sounds like a radical form of free expression, but unfortunately it is merely another form of that discredited affirmationism, 'positive thinking' (see Fritz for a thorough deconstruction). 'Opposition – thinking differently – is a necessity. However, not every rebellion is genuine, and not every opposition is thinking' (Peperzak).

THE PUPPET SHOW

Taoism finds a parallel in the West through perhaps unexpected means, including that simplest form of children's entertainment, the puppet show. Heinrich von Kleist's *On the Puppet Theater* (1810) presented a discourse that was philosophically close to Taoism, contending that the spontaneous movement of puppets is superior to that of trained dancers; a mechanically-controlled puppet doesn't resort to the distortion of thought but acts without calculation or self-consciousness, the way of effortless action.

The equivalent of a Taoist puppet show was, believe it or not, *Sooty and Sweep*, a silent magic-conjuring bear and his slightly demonic sidekick, a black and white TV analogue image evocation at the hearth or possibly even north-east corner (where the demons enter) of 1960s British homes. It supplanted radio and earlier direct parental story-telling which may also have included puppets. Literally right- and left-handed representations of 'good' and 'naughty', the mediating influence between the magically silent Sooty and noisome Sweep (what better names for hearth deities) was Soo (a panda it should be noted, and the embodiment of the Mysterious Female). With the puppeteer Harry Corbett albeit unwittingly playing the role of a *Tao-shih* (his surname derives from the French *corbet*, raven, which in

Chinese myth is a messenger of the gods) and presenting such lessons as magic being hard work that sometimes leads to unexpected results, it's tempting to think a covert Taoist puppetry was surreptitiously a part of my childhood.

'You, darkness that I come from,
I love you more than all the fires
that fence the world,
for the fire makes a circle of light for everyone,
and then no one outside learns of you,
But the darkness pulls in everything,
shapes and fires, animals and myself.
How easily it gathers them,
powers and people.
And it is possible a great energy is moving near us.
I have faith in nights.'
Rainer Maria Rilke, *You, Darkness*

THE REVEREND Hampden C. DuBose, a missionary in China in the 19th Century, wrote an entertaining summation of the collective wisdom of Chinese thought: 'The "Dragon" is the emblem of China and its State Church; the "Image" is a synonym for the Indian religion – it matters little the size, colour or name of the image; and the term "Demon" is Taoism in a nut-shell.' It is revealing that his impression of Taoism was demonic, because at the current time the Tao is rather embraced in the extreme as all that is light and vague, and has been consigned to the New Age Spirituality section of bookshops.

To counterbalance that view does not require an inversion of its values but a fair evaluation of the inner dimension of what can be termed the 'Demonic' or 'shadow' aspect of Tao in all its manifestations: philosophically, religiously, mystically and magically.

Shadow magic – as used to describe working with actual shadows as spirits in conjuration, or as the term may be found in some popular entertainments – is very distinct from *Ying Mo* (*Shadow Magic*) as Taoist practice. In order to see how the Shadow is presented, we will turn to some of the classic texts in the Tao-tsang (Taoist Canon).

Woven throughout the early philosophical foundation of Taoism (*Tao-chia*) is the notion of the Yin element of shadows and darkness as positive force, as can be seen in the *Chuang-tzu*. Chuang Tzu (c. 369-286 BCE) was a founder of philosophical Taoism along with Lao Tzu (c. 6th Century BCE). The *Chuang-tzu* consists of 33 chapters; the first seven, the 'inner' books, were actually written by Chuang-tzu, the rest is believed to be the work of his disciples. He writes with wonderful insight and a deceptive simplicity on the human condition, besides being refreshingly down to earth and humorous.

In the two stories below, the Shadow of the first is to one man a demon, but in the second tale the Shadow itself is haunted by a questioning ghost. Chuang-tzu uses the name Wangliang (Wangliang interprets as 'demon') for his character Penumbra, and Jing, 'bright', for Shadow. The *Chuang-tzu* was not considered a scripture of the Canon until the T'ang dynasty.

Flight from the Shadow

There once was a man who was frightened by his own shadow and scared of his own footprints. So he tried to escape them by running away. But every time he lifted his foot and brought it down, he made more footprints. And no matter how fast he ran, his shadow never left him. Thinking he must be running too slowly, he ran faster and faster until, exhausting himself, he collapsed and died. He had no idea that by sitting in the shade and resting quietly, he would have lost his shadow and ceased to make footprints.

The Penumbra and the Shadow

The Penumbra asked the Shadow, 'Formerly, you were walking on, and now you have stopped; formerly you were sitting, and now you have risen up – how is it that you are so without stability?' The Shadow replied, 'I wait for the movements of something else to do what I do, and that something else on which I wait waits further on another to do as it does. My waiting, is it for the scales of a snake, or the wings of a cicada? How should I know why I do one thing, or do not do another?'

In the *Lao Tzu* (*Tao te Ching, The Way and its Power*), the Spirit of the Valley is the dark shadow force, 'there within us all the while'. Lao Tzu, also known as Lao Tan and Li Erh, was a contemporary of Confucius (6th Century BCE). It is not now believed that the *Tao Te Ching* was written before the 4th or 3rd centuries. The *Lao-tzu* was not a scriptural text as there were other sources of revelation.

'The Valley Spirit never dies.
It is named the Mysterious Female
And the doorway of the Mysterious Female
Is the base from which Heaven and Earth sprang.
It is there within us all the while.
Draw upon it as you will, it never runs dry'.
Tao Te Ching, Chapter VI. Translation by Arthur Waley.

Chaos, darkness and obscurity are 'the substance of the Great Life' in Chapter 21, referred to by the alchemists. 'Chaotic and dark are its images.' These books offer the advice of people, not that of deities, which presumably is one reason they are not afforded the same degree of veneration as religious texts in other traditions.

In 'The Conference of the Birds', the Sufi Farid al-din 'Attar describes the path of the mystic as proceeding through seven valleys: the Valley of the Quest, of Love, Knowledge, Detachment, Unity, Bewilderment and finally Annihilation. The Valley obviously has an inverse property in contrast to a mountain as a spiritual retreat. A valley is passed through, whereas a mountain is conquered.

The empty circle at the bottom of the *wu-chi* diagram (see 'Diagram of the Supreme Ultimate', p.114) is the Mysterious Gate, or the Valley Spirit (*Gu Shen* or *Ku Shen*), which in esoteric physiology resides in the *ming-men* (life gate) located on the spine between the kidneys. The Spirit of the Valley has been interpreted as an actual deity, identified with the Primordial Mother Hsuan-p'in, representing the Tao in herself or, with *ku* interpreted as mountain spring, possibly a deity of springs. The Valley Spirit can be seen as a description of

Emptiness in a positive form, supporting life, providing shade and, just as a valley channels the flow of water, directing energy. Yin energy is here expressed as the Mysterious Female: the Life Force, the Dark Female, the root of what may be manifested.

In *The Mystical Theology* of Dionysius the Areopagite, or Pseudo-Dionysius as he is also known, 'the Divine Darkness' stands for the supreme source of all. The 'immutable mysteries of theology are veiled in the dazzling obscurities of the secret Silence, out-shining all brilliance with the intensity of their Darkness.' And, 'We pray that we may come unto this Darkness which is beyond light.'

According to St. John of the Cross, the highest form of contemplation is not in light but rather darkness – a 'Dark Contemplation'. Because Western thought has tended broadly to the analytical rather than holistic or synthetic, the view of that which opposes has been framed as an antagonism. Christianity for example personifies evil as 'The Opposer'. The Yin-Yang concept is by contrast a philosophy of accommodation.

Yin-Yang, meaning 'dark and sunny side' of a hill, symbolizes the two complementary forces composing all universal phenomena. Yin represents earth, the female, rest, darkness. Also, even numbers, the valley, the broken line. Yang is male, heaven, light, activity, odd numbers, the unbroken line, the mountain. (The assignment of gender can be misleading; we will return to that issue later). The principle was first mentioned in a 4th Century appendix to the *I Ching*, where it is said, 'A succession of Yin and Yang is called the Tao'. The Huainanzi, a 2nd Century BCE collection of essays by scholars in the employ of Liu An, prince of Huainan, describes how Primordial Qi (*Yuan Qi*) divided into the Yang breath forming Heaven, and the Yin breath which formed Earth. Through a continuing diversification the Ten Thousand Things were produced.

A school of thought was devoted to this precept in the 3rd Century BCE, and over time it has influenced art, divination, medicine, even government, continuing into the present where it is employed in social theory and even molecular biology; see for example respectively Tony Fang's *Yin-Yang: A New Perspective on Culture* and Hua Lu's *p53 and MDM2: their Yin-Yang intimacy*.

The principle of duality as being supportive for our psychological wellbeing was proposed by Carl Gustav Jung, who gained many of his insights through a study of Eastern philosophies. Taoism as a philosophy that can be combined with psychological therapies and theories has become a recognised source of inspiration for some in the mental health professions; *Shadow and Individuation in China* as one illustration is a summary of presentations by Dr. John Beebe at an International Conference of Analytical Psychology.

For Jung, duality was a fact of nature. Integrating the dark side of the self is a necessity for achieving wholeness. The Shadow is the archetype for this dark side, which needs to be acknowledged, confronted and synthesized. Anima and animus (female and male personality aspects), along with the rational (thought and feeling) and irrational (sensing, intuition) components require balancing.

Taking a quick glance at another culture's view, the ancient Egyptian concept of soul components which included the personality (*Ba*), the vital energy equivalent to Qi (*Ka*), the physical heart (*Ib*), and the name (*Ren*) also considered the *Sheut* or Shadow as an essential aspect, containing a measure of the individual's identity that made an impact on the world. In Egypt, a land of intense sun and so consequently sharply defined shadows, this is perhaps particularly understandable.

Trying to ignore or suppress the Shadow, the Demonic, takes energy and causes imbalance. Harmony within oneself is the result of Individuation, or the practice of coherence. This is facilitated by paying attention to the realm of symbol and metaphor. It can be a fearful and pain-filled experience. The Shadow as the dark side of personality is unconscious, a counterpoint to the persona or conscious ego. It consists of negative or primitive impulses and emotions such as lust and anger, selfishness and greed. It is denied expression through its unacceptability. The archetypal, rather than personal shadow is a transpersonal evil, symbolized by demons.

Jung in one sense used the term Shadow as a construct corresponding to demonic possession, and as a primordial, ancestral and inherited part of our whole identity. In denial of what is within, this demonic aspect is projected outward onto individuals, nations, religions. The Adversary outside is the opposite of what we perceive to be Right, a dissociation from the sub-personality within. Personal accountability and the realisation of our projections is necessary in order to gain our own power and moral well-being. By rejecting responsibility for the Shadow, we categorise it as an extraneous and uncontrollable force. However, the Shadow has its positive aspect because it is not irredeemable.

'Who knows what evil lurks in the hearts of men? The Shadow knows.'
(From the 1930s pulp comic and radio show).

Following Steven A. Diamond's observations on the close complement of the Demonic with the Creative, that destructiveness is not far removed from intense creative expression, the 'Creative Orientation' as Robert Fritz has called it can channel the Demonic within oneself. This tension of opposites is what Fritz has utilised in his concept of Structural Tension, where the difference between having and not-having, or an unrealised goal and its accomplishment, is used practically in order to achieve ambitions.

Although the concept of wholeness and the traditional teachings on the attainment of enlightenment or self-realisation are ascribed to a state of non-duality, we are limited by our dualistically conditioned intellect, and non-duality is only a model for an awakened state. 'Oneness' leads to absence, denial rather than involvement in life and a joyful participation in the interplay of duality. Believing the world in its polarity is unreal, and that only the principle of non-duality (the Sanskrit term *Advaita* translates as 'Not two') is a fitting representation of ultimate reality, excuses inactivity and passivity. We should not be coerced into thinking that more information is equivalent to more enlightenment.

This is where the 'New Age' movement has been led astray. Its 'Waves of Information' focus on 'Light' and 'Light Workers' meant the complementary Dark has been denied as anathema to spiritual evolution. The Demonic has been done a grave disservice.

Fear of the Unknown haunts us superstitiously, or at the other extreme we are immersed in blank materialism – afraid of our own Shadow, as the saying goes. We fear the dark even though more cases of supernatural activity such as the encountering of ghosts are reported during the day than at night. According to esoteric teaching, the spine-tingling sensation associated with fear and experiences of alternate reality is actually indicating an energetic prompting apart from a primal instinct of 'what's behind you'; evolutionary energy travels upward along the spinal column passing energetic 'gates' that have been assiduously catalogued by Taoist internal-school alchemists over time.

The Void or the Abyss, termed as *Wu Chi* by the Chinese or *Ain Soph Aur* by the Qabalists, the Great Unmanifest, is held as an initial stage of creation, a *potentia*, implying something from nothing. This nullity has an equivalence to God, a deity forming the world out of inexpressible non-content. It exists in absentia.

These koan-like concepts and paradoxes take us to the edge of some ultimate truth, just as shedding or losing our preconceptions brings us to the edge of the personal desert, the emptiness where we question what is real/unreal and how we represent what cannot be represented: the theoretical limitlessness that can result in a philosophy of dissolution. To return to a virgin state of emptiness is behind the tyrant's Year Zero, to wipe the slate clean and remove memory – annihilation as the means of a return to Eden. The 'War on Terror' is a phrase loaded with its own sense of absurdity, as is a current affectation, that of 'Existential Threat' (or amusingly enough, E.T.).

Opposition then is not, to the Taoist, a question of struggle. In the usual sense, an opposing force must be met with resistance; it is alienated and outlawed. Tribalism, nationalism, and any other divisiveness result from not logically accepting that taking a position necessitates an opposite point. Argument and criticism are the lifeblood of development in most endeavours. The Other is demonised through an erroneous desire for uniformity. As Mikhail Bulgakov questioned; '...what would the earth look like if all the shadows disappeared?'

The all too apparent corollary of demonising women by association with the 'dark' of Yin does not display an understanding of the real correspondence as complementarity. Gender translates as *xingbie* in Chinese; it is a difference of individual nature, a difference that correlates through a dynamic interaction. Yin and Yang are actually not specifically related to gender. The characteristic of dichotomizing male and female in favour of a masculine hierarchy has been a disastrous phenomenon throughout cultures globally. In fact, male/female, Yin/Yang qualities are fluid, and would be recognisably part of all individual experience and self-expression in an enlightened society.

While Chinese social tradition was (and in all truth still is) largely sexist, Taoist and even some Confucian texts promote 'the feminine' positively, though we should not read these texts in the light of modern ideas of feminism; the exchange of one extreme for another is not conducive to the true Way of balance and harmony.

OVERSHADOWING

Overshadowing has a negative connotation in analytical psychology. In our usage it denotes a guiding shadow, or entity. An exercise involving two people facing each other and staring fixedly at one another's faces, preferably by a low light, is one method alleged to reveal an overshadow, similar to the solo practice of gazing into a mirror. (Optical illusion or eye-strain is the rationalist explanation, bluntly missing the magic through its haste to explain the trick.) Hypnotic depth regression is another psychosynthetic form of potentially contacting an entity, if not even an alternate self. This is not anything to do with 'Walk-ins', the New Age idea of souls taking over vacated bodies, like squatters.

To return again to a quote from Rilke, a dark contemplator if there ever was one, 'If my devils leave me, my angels will too.' Though to Rilke, every angel was terrifying as well. (Tennessee Williams is also credited with the quote, as 'If I got rid of my demons, I'd lose my angels too' – angels being in most sources a far cry from the prissy feathery beings of popular depiction.) Angels, especially the common or Guardian variety, don't translate into Taoist counterparts.

A General Perspective of the Demonic

'The shadow escapes from the body like an animal we had been
sheltering'. Gilles Deleuze
(*Francis Bacon, The Logic of Sensation*)

THE WESTERN cultural representation of demons in film and print,
and its magical tradition procedures of evocation or exorcism, tends
to follow a narrow parameter which may have certain points in
common with the Eastern, but is not in total accordance, and certainly
should not be taken as definitive. The experience of contact with the
demonic through, say, the grimoires is not equivalent to the Taoist's
interaction, with his or her magical medium being the physical body.

To make a comparison, it's the difference between writing an
algebraic formula and shamanic dancing on a pub table. Or, cold
calling and extending a polite open invitation. Now, let's take a look
at some common presentations of demon kind.

Demons have been interpreted as personal guides, guardian
spirits and messengers. The original Greek word *daimon* was not a
negative term but meant *spirit* or *divine power* and was used by Plato to
define Socrates' inspiration. (Some scholars have considered whether
Socrates suffered a form of epilepsy, as descriptions of his state of
communion with his daimon are comparable to the condition.) It
can also be defined simply as 'to know'. Demons are thus intelligent
beings. *Eudaimonia* means *good spiritedness*. It might be said that the
ancient Greeks were working out a psychology of attributing internal
forces as agencies.

A demon however came to be considered an unclean spirit when
the pagan cult statues inhabited by their gods' presence became seen
as unwholesome. This shift to malicious attribution derived from late
Roman culture. In other cultures too the demonic has an association
with dark forces; Buddhism, Islam and the other religions or offshoots
all pay attention to the demonic realm, sometimes with elaborate
gratification. The demon is then a malevolent spirit, the daimon or
daemon a benevolent one.

Persian Zoroastrian dualism was influential on Judaism in the identification of demons with a dedicated evil, headed by Satan (See Russell quoted in McCraw and Arp). The Abrahamic religions each have a constituent demonology. Concrete being or allegory, demons as a category of entity between gods and humans can be analysed as not necessarily negative but 'value-neutral'. (The djinn as intermediate beings between humanity and divinity were formed from smoke-free flame, humans from clay, angels from light.) Similarly, possession may not be a bad experience. Exorcism therefore depends on context.

The New Testament is crowded with tales of demonic possession, as, it might be surmised, a platform from which to promote the character of Jesus as healer/exorcist. The authority of Christ was made clear by his power over demons, and that revelatory process included the performance of miracles. In the simple division of Good and Evil, the Christian God allows demons to do evil in order to test faith, with Satan tormenting Job and numerous demons attacking St. Anthony as examples. But God is still complicit in these malevolent acts, having instigated them, which makes His (it is a He according to this doctrinal path) nature dualistic.

In the Age of Reason, Descartes' demon became a device for illustrating an argument, a conjuration of a non-existent world of hallucination and doubt. The heretical position was to view the world of *Reality* as a demonic creation, reality as illusion being a Manichaeistic conjecture.

As a deflection from self-responsibility demons serve a valuable aid; here they are psychic conditions, where an energy or complex is possessing the subject rather than an actual entity. The clichés of the 'demon drink', or drugs, and the expression of 'dealing with personal demons' are about autonomous complexes, the unconsciousness of fixed ideas. Demons are not obsolete, they have just taken on another form. We are possessed now by complexes.

This psychological interpretation sees demons as unresolved or emerging negative aspects of the self, which may be resolved or integrated back into the personality, sometimes with an enhanced sense of self-knowledge. Freud's explanation in *Totem and Taboo* was of demons and spirits being projections of emotions for the primeval (I would rather avoid the term 'primitive') comprehension.

The 'Dweller on the Threshold', a term used in Edward Bulwer-Lytton's *Zanoni*, represents the creature Dante is confronted by in his Purgatorio, 'Una Lonza', a guardian between the worlds. Here we have an instance of the Positive Demonic, an entity that presents on the surface as evil but which in effect has a protective function, to warn of dangers. The Negative Demonic does not exhibit that level of care.

Further inhabitants of the human constitution seeking resolution include the 'inner beast' we could define as separate from the Dweller, and the 'Double-goer' or doppelganger as aspect of the Shadow, our 'dark passenger', each of which could be perceived as a remnant of an older current of cerebral development.

The magical Astral form (e.g. Tulpa, see David-Neel) which may be encountered by others as if real is a vehicle for the projected self, or an exteriorisation phenomenon, though it may not contain the full consciousness of the individual. The outward projection of an opposing form is utilised in martial arts as a point of focus; this is an example of internal applications of external arts such as shadow boxing.

As a martial technique, contact with and employment of these aspects is recorded in shamanic tales of shape-shifting, such as the early Chinese shaman/chieftain Yu who could transform into a bear, reminding us that the term for the wild Norse warriors, the Berserkers, comes from bear-sark, or bear shirt.[1] The Filipino martial art of Kuntao also has a shape-shifting practice, as do the training methods of the Russian special forces Systema. The engagement of the oldest part of the brain, the Reptilian, as a fighting technique effecting a change in personality is considered to be a component of martial styles and posture.[2] The Dragon/Reptile is an archetype commonly invoked in fighting.

The Double or Shadow is an indicator of the essential nature of Tao as binary system. Western demons lost their astringency over time, as such horrors as the Inquisition and two World Wars presented the unquestionable ability of humans to be capable of more evil towards each other than demons could match. If hell is life on earth for many then what fears can the afterlife afford?

---

1   Professor Brondsted notes that 'bare sark' is another interpretation, i.e. 'shirtless' which he defines as 'without armour'. He mentions 'other fanatical fighters', ulfhednar, 'wolfskins'.

2   See Montaigue on the 'C' back posture, in *Dim-Mak: Death-Point Striking*, p.40

The Unseen

"'All I know is, I kept bumping into things,' said the King.'
James Thurber.

An original trait of *gui* was that they were unseen. Eventually their depiction was too enticing a prospect to artists. However, the demonic world which cannot be seen but is suggested is a more terrifying prospect than that which is openly presented (as can be experienced in watching some films such as *The Haunting*). For practicing magicians, invisibility is a coveted power, alongside the ability to fly. For most other people invisibility is something to be feared. Especially their own.

Making things disappear, whether they are alive or inanimate, is a favourite trick of conjurors (and politicians); the necessity of making them reappear is to pacify the audience (or electorate), who would otherwise be left with the disturbance of a death experience. No one presumably wants to be discreetly confronted with their own mortality as an entertainment, although it works as an indiscreet confrontation for amusement park rides.

One of the collections of magical techniques for Taoist adepts was *A Chart of the Magic Art of Being Invisible* by an anonymous author or authors, and which has only survived in fragments from the late Han Dynasty. Anonymity is its own form of invisibility and was practiced by many Taoists writing instructive texts. It was further a form of self-detachment, a freedom from ego.

The Qimen Dunjia system and magical invisibility is mentioned later, in the chapter on Circle Walking. Being able to conceal the physical form indicates entering another dimension, a supernatural quality that will bring us to the attention of the inhabitants of that dimension, spirits and/or demons, through raising ourselves to their level. It may indicate as well being shadowless, as there is no apparent form to cast a shadow. On the other hand, the shadow may be all there is to be seen.

To become Unseen is to be outside the world of Resistance, the world subject to natural laws. To enter an Otherworld, or to be Unworldly, is to thereby identify ourselves as Spirit beings. Psychologically the attraction of not being apparent is a wish to retreat from the world, or a sense of fear in being truly seen. Mostly individuals now seek a converse position of being universally observed – 'fame' for its own sake. Extraversion seems to be in the ascendant over the Yin position of Introversion.

The unseen is a source of fear. Demons are emblematic of the peculiar and particular guidance afforded by fear, even terror, which has its own quality of initiation, revelation and personal confrontation. It addresses our sense of survival, control and protection. Instincts may be sharpened or paralysed by a demon emerging into consciousness and the most powerful initiatory processes can involve the instigation of fear as a 'feint at death'.

There are a variety of methods for allegedly producing the effect of invisibility, including the sets of hand forms that are described later in the book. Meditation instils a kind of invisibility – physical stillness to the point of becoming immersed in our setting. An early primer in my education in things 'occult' was J. H. Brennan's *Experimental Magic*, which culminated with a chapter on 'Ritual Invisibility'. It very helpfully included an appendix titled 'Regaining Visibility'.

The attribute of becoming invisible obviously appeals to our demonic side; what could we get away with if no one knew we were there? H. G. Wells insisted upon a Hollywood script for his *Invisible Man* that would recognise it was not the formula which made his protagonist insane, but the state of being invisible itself.

Occultism, translated as what is hidden, from the Latin root *occultus*, has entered a redundant phase (a controversial notion, but I'll present it), because with the advent of free access to all information, nothing is hidden. It, whatever it may be, is all out there. If indeed everyone is now special, then what is the adolescent magician to do to make themself observed in their own dark mirror?

There is a concerted assault on secrecy right now (for the citizen, not the State). It turns us inside out. Thought policing regards privacy as suspect; all must be observed. Omnipresent filming, the recording of each experience into a revisited visual condensation, is our compact with the demon of images. 'To Know' became demonic, so too has 'To Be Unseen' once more. At the same time our other senses are in abeyance, with plastic surfaces dulling our sense of touch, artificial scents such as air 'purifiers' contaminating our sense of smell, and so on; there is an emphasis on the visually palpable. A proliferation of imagery overloading and unbalancing our sensory input, Appearance is at once condemnatory and celebratory, while Disappearance is an accusation: 'the Disappeared' are victims of political violence. Or, they are the Old.

As the symbol of the Bagua denotes the cycle of life, the final trigram is 'Mountain'. The retreat to the mountain was the allegorical transcendence of the Taoist adept to the quality of invisibility, or death. In the end, the last stage of our alchemical journey, we all become invisible. Hopefully we still retain our presence in other ways.

TOWARDS THE OTHER SIDE

Further to the suggestion of a Taoist social conscience made in the introduction, a duty of Taoist social care is exorcising illusion. The contrivance of governments is making the inconvenient vanish. Veneration of age as indicative of wisdom through experience is at a far remove from certain societies' virtual condemnation of aging, where the old are perceived as no longer valid, are institutionalised in care homes or generally disregarded and thus made unseen. The constancy of change, and its acceleration, with emphasis placed on the New (which often translates as novelty rather than necessarily anything profound) means by association 'the cult of Youth' is valued more than Age. Ageism as a politically-correct observance is paid lip-service, but regardless of this the old are condemned by a view that they have outlived their utility; in 2013 the UK's Health Secretary Jeremy Hunt called the country's treatment of the elderly a 'national shame'.

Chinese culture has always fostered a tradition of respect towards the aged, with a resistance to placing family members in care homes. The Communist Party's one-child policy is altering the structure of the family, and along with this more people are living for longer. How this will impact on tradition remains to be seen. The Chinese sage retreating to a mountain to transform to something other is an act of dignified mystique; the old transformed by collective neglect into an alienated otherness, devoid of dignity, is unfortunately a by-product of the growing inhumanism resulting from possession by technology. The urge to exorcise age is evident in cosmetic treatments which merely result in a mask.

Relating to the matter of death reveals itself by our fear of shadows and what cannot be seen. Inversely, because the old are that much nearer to the great mystery, in our society they can tend to be relegated from any position of attention. This is consequent of how inadequate the connection to spirituality has become, lost through materialism and a focus on the world of appearances.

The alchemy of transition to being non-apparent as a respected coda to earthly existence will be made easier by a societal attitude change, and when ageing is no longer demonised. The most frightening conditions of old age are still turned into demons, much as some diseases were thought to be the work of demonic influence in the middle ages; 'The Demons of Dementia' was the title of an article in The Lancet in 2009.

'This invisibility has its drawbacks after all.' (Tolkien)

THE CONCEPT OF EVIL

'The worst evils are committed not by monsters, but people
no different from ourselves.' Lars Svendsen.

Understanding what evil is, its nature, is summarized by Plotinus: 'Those inquiring whence Evil enters into beings, or rather into a certain order of beings, would be making the best beginning if they established first of all what precisely Evil is' (*Enneads*, I, 8 1). As categorized by Svendsen (*A Philosophy of Evil*), there are four types: Demonic (unalloyed evil), Instrumental (where the ends justify the means), Idealistic (with evil acts being committed in the belief they are good, such as the witch trials) and Stupid (ignorance, acting thoughtlessly).

Explanations or observations have ranged from Manichaean dualism, through the Neoplatonist theory of 'lack' or privation, to Kant's idea that evil is a flaw of the will, and to Hannah Arendt's report on 'the banality of evil' (*Eichmann in Jerusalem*).

Evil in the understanding of the Taoist is an effect of human action being in opposition to the Tao. As cause and consequence, it follows from human will. This is not to say human will itself is evil. That depends on whether it is directed harmfully. Evil is not said to exist in nature from Lao Tzu's reading of it, although Chuang Tzu recognises there being suffering in nature as an effect of change, which should be philosophically accepted. Nature is amoral. The problem of evil is to be resolved in this life as a necessity of dualism, recognising such and embracing *wu-wei* (the Taoist concept of natural action), rather than postponing its resolution to the afterlife.

The principle of Yin may be associated with evil but not to an extent of classifying everything under its categorisation, such as women, as evil, unlike in purely dualistically-bounded views. Keep in mind that the category is not absolute but transmutable. Good and evil are not in opposition but rely on the same essential source. Goodness may come from cultivation; badness may result from losing virtue.

In Chinese symbols of evil, 'one-legged' is an attribute of a certain demon, or class of demon. This does not refer to a crass association of deformity with 'wrongness', as with James Bond villains whose facial scars or artificial hands are outward indicators of inner badness in contrast to the physical perfection of the hero. Having one leg, and/or difficulties in walking such as a limp, reflect a chthonic origin. Learning to walk upright on two legs is an evolutionary process. The force of evolution is also portrayed by the dragon.

Waylun Lai in *Symbolism of Evil in China* notes that the Emperor K'ung-chia of the Hsia dynasty, who could be called China's Adam, was born a dragon but lost his *te* (virtue). In forgetting his dragonic essence, in failing to nurture that essence in him, this first man died a man and came down in China's history as an 'evil king'. Here we see that the dragon is not an evil symbol but one denoting a virtuous power.

Good and Evil as absolutes may have fallen out of favour and been replaced with relativism, but the two constructs are still generally recognisable in human affairs. With humanism taking over from religious attributions, demons as culpable for human misbehaviour is not a widely indulged defence, however the extremism now evident in every sphere of life means Good and Evil have been resurrected as viable concepts. The politics of extremism makes division more clearly defined, as with National Populism pitted against Liberal Democracy. One extreme invokes another, the Physics of Tao prescribing for every action an equal and opposite reaction. Newton was surely moved by the spirit of the Way.

The place of Taoism in this, as values of Right and Wrong emerge from the fog of moral relativism, is that if it does not provide resolution it can at least present understanding.

Chinese demons are not always such mindlessly malicious creatures. They may have characters that waver between good and evil. Some have supporters among tribal communities who render them with purpose; Chi You for one is either war hero or war demon according to tribal affiliation. In fact, there is a fabulous literature of fictive Chinese demons. Chinese Gods and Demons fiction, *Shenmo xiaoshuo*, first appeared in the Ming Dynasty and is still extant in a range of media from comic books to internet gaming. In *The Journey to the West* we find – to name a few: Baigujing, the shape-shifting skeleton spirit; Niumowang, the Bull Demon King and his brother, Immortal Ruyi; the Demon King of Confusion; the Black Wind and the Yellow Wind Demons; the trio of General Yin, Xiong Shanjun and Techu Shi; the Yellow Robed Demon; the Golden and Silver Horned Kings; the Lion-Lynx Demon; the Tuolong or Water Lizard Dragon; the Immortals of Tiger, Elk and Antelope Power; the Single Horned Rhinoceros King; the Scorpion Demon and the Python Demon; Sai Tai Sui, the steed of Guan Yin; the Seven Spider Demons; the Hundred Eyed Demon Lord; and on the list goes. This array was a reflection of actual demonographies with their similarly colourful characteristics.

The First Century BCE catalogue in the royal Han library included demonographies to identify spirits along with magical techniques to control them. Harper (see *A Chinese Demonography of the Third Century BC*) lists some of these lost books, including: *Portentous and Propitious Mutant Prodigies*; *Declarations of Odium for Mutant Prodigies* and *Seizing the Unpropitious and Subjugating Spectral Entities*. The text of *Chieh* ('Chieh' interprets as investigation or interrogation, or spell-binding) on a bamboo manuscript from a 3rd century BCE tomb at Shui-hu-ti in Hupei contains about 70 separate entries of 'demonic harassment' with remedies. The manuscripts also include the Pace of Yu ritual walk, found as well in the Mawangdui manual of medicine, the *Wu-shih-erh ping fang* (*Recipes for 52 Ailments*), exorcistic methods to dispel disease-demons. The *Pao p'u tzu* lists the *Record of Nine Cauldrons* (*Chiu ting chi*) as a document used to drive demons away. Another talismanic book was the *Shan hai ching*, which listed habitats of earth spirits.

Illustrated: The first ten slips of the 'Chieh' text, reproduced from *Yun-meng Shui-hu-ti Ch'in mu*. Plates 131-132.
(The Chinese editors have placed their transcription to the left of each slip of the original manuscript).

The Christian binary opposition of Good versus Evil was introduced by the Jesuits in their Chinese catechism *Tianzhu shilu* (*The Veritable Record of the Lord of Heaven*) in 1584. They had noted that Chinese officials were afraid of demons and the view was they were everywhere in nature, as coming from the Five Elements, as essences of mountains, rivers, animals, stones and plants, and by virtue of natural transformation rather than divine instigation.

The Christian faith in China was cannily promoted through exorcism, and even the Chinese gods were turned into demons. Taoist and Buddhist texts, idols and manuals of divination were destroyed as demonic. One of the missionaries, John Livingstone Nevius, collected accounts of possession, and also recorded his personal experiences, in *Demon Possession and Allied Themes* (1895). Curiously, for Chinese demons, they all responded to the Christian form of exorcism.

REPTILIANS ARE WATCHING YOU

Graffiti, Granada

'Demons may be good or bad, like any other class of beings'.
L. Frank Baum.[3]

THE CREATOR Gods Fuxi and Nuwa are depicted as serpent beings intertwined caduceus-like. The serpent-dragon has an ambiguous or ambivalent nature. Zhulong or Zhuyin, the red solar dragon, also had a snake's body with a human face. By opening and closing its eyes it created day and night. There is a totemic correlation of snake, fish and dragon as dwellers in the deep. The dragon encompassed all beings originally: reptilian, mammalian, aquatic and avian.

Reptilian/human forms may represent a subconscious image of a resolved whole; the concept of the 'Reptilian brain' contains our more tenebrous qualities. In mythologies around the world there is a blending of human and serpent; the first king of Athens, Cecrops I, was mythically half man and half snake. Other examples are the Chinese Dragon Kings, Glycon the snake god, the Lamia and the Gorgons, Ningishzidda or Ningizzida, ancestor of Gilgamesh represented as two snakes around a rod or a serpent with a human head. Xiangliu or Xiangyou is a nine-headed snake monster with human faces. One

---

3 Baum, author of *The Wonderful Wizard of Oz*, was a member of the Theosophist Society, and knew a thing or two about magic and the spirit world.

of the formulas known to esoteric circles for evoking or invoking a reptilian energy is that of IAO, a serpent-faced entity, which we will explore later in the section dealing with alchemical exercises.

The Serpent is dualistic, both good and evil. Its venom can heal or kill, and it is connected to immortality by its ability to shed its skin. The Genesis narrative has a serpent wrapped around the Tree of the Knowledge of Good and Evil, i.e. The Tree of Duality. The Serpent is the purveyor of this knowledge.

Fu Xi and Nüwa, Anonymous, 4th-8th c.

Further great psychomythic symbols include the Hydra, the Rainbow Serpent, the ouroboros, the Midgard serpent and the Dragon Lines channelling energy through the earth. In the Book of Revelation, the giant seven-headed dragon is Satan. The Egyptian deity Sebek is represented as having a human form and a crocodile's head.

Chinese emperors were supposedly living dragons. The Dragon Kings are related to the Four Directions, Four Cardinal Points and the Four Seas. Chinese dragons are a cultural symbol without the European association of fire-breathing aggression, and date back thousands of years. They represent evolution and personal energy (qi). There is a warning not to mark oneself with the sign of a dragon (such as a tattoo) unless having permission from the Dragon Lords.

David Icke has, unfortunately I feel, propagated a myth of the 'shape-shifting reptoid alien' as a force of evil, possessing heads of state and corporate leaders. Once again this deflects the attention from the fact that humans need not have an excuse of demonic possession to demonstrate greed and selfishness. It ties into the fear side of our fascination with reptiles; we are either repelled or entranced, but either way intrigued. The *Jurassic Park* film series continues to be big box-office. This is because there is an undeniable deep-seated connection, a kind of innate familiarity.

Reptilian aliens get a bad press; they are a projection of a misunderstood identification. That Icke projects this image onto the British Royal Family provides a subconscious clue: The Royal Way is a term for alchemy.

Essentially the Reptilians (theoretically speaking of course) are more likely to be guides to evolution. The Yogic Kundalini, the 'Serpent Power', spiralling around the spinal column as shown in the caduceus, is a form of energy awakened to lead to higher consciousness. (It notoriously can also lead reputedly to 'Kundalini psychosis', or 'burnt-out hippy' syndrome.)

There is now criticism of the 'Triune Brain' and 'R-complex' (reptilian complex) theory. Paul MacLean applied Plato's concept of the psyche as consisting of three parts (*logistikon*, *thumos* and *epithymia*: rational thoughts, emotions or 'passions' and instinctual drives such as hunger and sex) to the cerebral, subcortical and limbic networks as an illustration of evolutionary progression; 'Lizard, Wolf and Human' has been another way of depicting this view. The reptilian brain was identified with fight or flight survivalism, aggression, anxiety, fear, territorialism and warfare – a demonic biological makeup. But the model of layers being added to the brain over time is not accurate; it is more of a holistic system with intricate cooperating connections, and so cannot be divided so neatly.

Nevertheless, there is an appeal to this primal sense of having a reptilian form buried deep inside us, which is perhaps why the theory is still in common use; it is a satisfying claim of progression through other forms to arrive at our present stage of development.

A few miles down the south-west coast of Cornwall from where I was born is The Lizard, a name which probably comes from the Cornish Lys Ardh, 'high court'. Coincidentally the rock in this location is serpentine, and there is a myth of the Lizard people having inhabited the area long ago, a particularly tall race. (The magic of most of the Kernewek landscape has unfortunately been eradicated by the predations of the tourist industry. Still, I digress; that is another tale and another cultural fable – the drowning of Lyonesse.)

Demons in Chinese Folklore

17th c. Painting by Lu Xue. *Zhong Kui with demons*.

CHINESE FOLK religion is the tradition of the Han people, entailing a veneration of nature and multiple deities, a metaphysical basis for Chinese thought that preserves aspects of shamanism and animism within local areas. These folk beliefs are woven through Taoism and vice versa, although there are naturally distinctions between the two.

There tends to be an ambivalent attitude in the Chinese traditions of supernatural classification toward the demonic. For example, plague demons could be called upon to protect communities. On the other hand there was also a categorisation and registering of demons more akin to the Western notion as being malevolent entities.

In Book II of Richard Wilhelm's translation of the I Ching, (*Ta Chuan/ The Great Treatise*, p.295), he comments that the spiritual forces that create visible existence belong either to the light or the dark. Light spirits (*shen*) are outgoing, active and can reincarnate. The dark spirits (*kuei*) return home, withdrawing with the task of assimilation of life experience.

This idea, of returning and outgoing by spirits of light and dark, does not signify a notion of good and evil beings; it is only an explanation or image of the expanding and the contracting life energy. This is reminiscent of Freud's notion of the Uncanny, bound to the death drive and The Return. The term for the Yin class of entities, *kuei* or *gui*, can also be interpreted therefore as 'contraction', and hence beings of chaos, with *shen* as expansion. In the Shuihudi demonography, symptoms of ill health are linked to demons, and instructions for cures supplied. Also, in the Huainanzi and the Guanzi, it is noted that the *qingji* or 'genie of the dry marsh' can be despatched by shouting its name and having it report back in a day.

The Physical world is a Yang condition, compared to the Yin state of the Spirit world. Humans are most comfortable in daylight (Yang), whereas spirits favour (mostly) the night. The Underworld, *Feng Du*, in comparison to the Celestial and Human realms contains the souls of the dead, ghosts and demons. It is ruled by Yang Luo Wang, and is a labyrinth of 18 levels. Upon death everyone passes into the Underworld through the Ghost Gate, where they are met by the guardians Ox-head and Horse-face and brought to the Three Judges of the Dead. The individual is either punished or rewarded according to the record of their life and eventually sent back to the material world. The Underworld is therefore not so much a Hell as Purgatory, although there are Hellish aspects to it.

The Festival of the Hungry Ghosts permits spirits to enter the land of the living until the sunrise of the following day. The seventh lunar month is the Ghost Month when the gates of hell are open. The Ghost Festival falls on the 15th day.

A main characteristic of demons in popular lore is their ability to transform into various forms – animals, plants, rocks (Maspero, *Taoism and Chinese Religion*, Book II). Given how *gui* can be translated between the two forms, not all demons are ghosts. Demons as human-like but not-human is a category-tension exacerbating the fear of confrontation with them.

Here are a few of the demons, ghosts and other assorted beings from Chinese folklore, which I have listed alphabetically:

Ba Jiao Gui: 'Banana ghost', a wailing female ghost living in a banana tree. Sometimes carries a baby. One tradition is to tie a red string around a tree trunk haunted by a Ba Jiao Gui, also sticking needles into the trunk, and tie the other end of the string to your bed. When the ghost appears at night asking to be set free the condition is made that they supply winning lottery numbers. If having won the ghost is still not freed, the gambler will meet a gruesome end.

Bai Gu Jing: White Bone Spirit. Appears in *Journey to the West*. The remains of a female corpse who can transform to her former beautiful self. Lives in a cave with her minions.

Bai Ze: A creature with a white body that can speak human languages and knows the name and appearance of every type of spirit and demon. Caught by the Emperor Huang Di, who asked it to record the forms of all demons and ghosts. Bai Ze wrote it on a scroll, the lost *Bai Ze Tu* or *Book of Bai Ze*.

Bi Fang: Giant bird resembling a crane that starts fires.

Bie You Ling: Turtle spirit whose upper body is that of a beautiful woman.

Chi mei: Mountain demon. Also, Chi is a hornless dragon.

Daji: Evil fox spirit in the novel *Investiture of the Gods* (*Fengshen Yanyi*). Possessed by a thousand-year-old vixen spirit, she became the concubine of King Zhou, last king of the Shang Dynasty, and took delight in torturing people.

Dao Lao Gui: Shoots poison darts at people.

Di Fu Ling: 'Earthbound Spirit'. Bound to places they had a strong connection to when living.

Diao Si Gui: Spirits who have either hanged themselves or been hanged. Depicted with long red tongues.

Diao Xue Gui: 'Hanging on Boots Ghost', follows people at night and plays pranks.

Dong Dong: A hybrid of a ram with a unicorn, with one eye, set behind an ear.

Du Jiao Gui Wang: 'Single Horned Demon King'. Features in *Journey to the West* as a friend of the Monkey King. His essence is concentrated in his horn.

E Gui: 'Hungry Ghost'. Appears during the Ghost Festival. The spirits of the greedy, they have green or grey skin and mouths too small to eat food. Insatiably hungry, they will consume anything, including rotting food and waste matter. The 'hungry ghosts' are those who died by hanging, drowning, a long way from home, or who have no ancestral tree.

E mo or **e sha**: Generic demon.

Fei: A plague monster with a bull's body, snake's tail and a third eye. Dries up rivers and marshes and withers grass and trees.

Fu Gui: Lives in the abdomen causing pain and eventual death.

Fu Yi Niao: A small bird with yellow fur and a red beak, its flesh can cure plague and parasites.

Gao Huang Gui: Lives in the area between the heart and diaphragm and causes physical and mental illness. Like the Fu Gui they have no physical description because, living in the body, they are never seen. The Chinese idiom about this being is *Xin zhong you gui*, 'to have a demon in one's heart'.

Gu Huo Niao: Bird demon that turns into a beautiful woman and snatches children away at night, having previously dotted their clothes with blood to mark the targets.

Gui: Spirits, ghosts, souls of the dead. Not necessarily demonic.

Gui Po: 'Old Woman Ghost'. May be the spirits of *amahs* (servants of rich families). Can be either helpful or evil.

Han Ba: Believed to be Pa, the drought fury.

Heibai Wuchang: 'Black and White Impermanence'. Two deities, one dressed in black, the other in white, who guide the spirits of the dead to the Underworld, being subordinates of its Lord, Yama. Sometimes represented as one being, Wuchang Gui, the 'Ghost of Impermanence'.

Hu Gui or **Hu Xian**, also **Huli Jing**: Friendly fox spirits. Not to be confused with fox demons, who are unfriendly. Can assume human form, and are generally female.

Hua Pi Gui: 'Painted Skin Ghost'. Green with big teeth but can also appear as beautiful women. Eat humans at night and wear the skins by day. They are the ghosts of wronged women whose spirits have remained for centuries in the bones of their corpses.

Hua Zhong Xian: A spirit who lives in a painting that has captured her image.

Huang Fu Gui: A shape shifter active in the Hubei area, appearing as mist, beasts or humans. Lecherous, lives on devouring other ghosts and can cause death or crippling injury with its hideous laughter.

Jian: Ghosts of ghosts.

Jiangshi: 'Stiff Corpse'. Chinese zombies. Have also in recent times assumed vampiric qualities, probably due to the influence of Western horror movies.

Jiu Tou Niao: A nine-headed bird-demon that sucks the spirit energy out of children.

Jiu wei hu: Nine-tailed fox spirit. Sounds like an infant. Eats people.

Kui: One-legged demon.

Lei: Bird like a magpie but with two heads and four claws. Extinguishes fires by flapping its wings.

Luo Tou Shi: Beings whose heads detach and fly off to wander around while they sleep.

Mao Gui: Ghost cat. Raised by Gu Du rituals (similar to Voodoo, or Hoodoo). Popular during the 6th and 7th centuries CE, when many cats were sacrificed for the purpose of using their spirits to target people. Mao Gui consume their victim's organs. The usual etymology search traces Moggy (or Moggie) to a derivation from Maggie as a pet's name, but just as Char comes from the Mandarin Cha for tea, I can't help but wonder whether Mao Gui is where we get the term 'Moggy' from.

Meng Po: Old Lady Meng, the Lady of Forgetfulness. She waits for the dead who are in line for reincarnation at the entrance of the 9th circle of Diyu, (the Chinese Hell, consisting of 18 circles and thus outnumbering Dante's version) and gives them the Five Flavoured Tea of Forgetfulness. This prevents them remembering their previous lives or their existence in hell.

Mogwai/Mogui: Inspiration for the *Gremlins* movie. Reproduce with the arrival of rain.

Niu Tou Man Mian: 'Ox-head and Horse-face', guardians of the Underworld. Their appearance is self-explanatory.

Nu Gui: Female ghost, in a red dress, sometimes white. The association with a red dress is due to her having worn one when she committed suicide. Returns to take revenge for an injustice. May also act as a succubus, seducing men and stealing their vital energy.

Nuba: A drought demon.

Pipa Jing: One of three female ghosts (with Daji and Splendour) who, under Nu Wa, disrupted the Shang Dynasty.

Sanshi: The Three 'Corpses' or Corpse-Demons, also known as the Three Worms (Sanchong), reside internally. Spiritual parasites with no permanent form, they live in the three *dantien* or energy centres of the body, and feed from grains. Their aim is to hasten the death of their host. A special diet was, or is, needed to eliminate them, along with Qi Gong exercises and leading a good and moral life. Because these demons are of especial interest in regard to the impact of agriculture historically as well as diet, I will return to them at the end of this chapter.

Shan Xiao or **shanxiao**: A monster/goblin that lives in the mountains. Is covered in fur and has large teeth. Can tear lions and tigers apart, has different guises and occasionally eats travellers. It has been posited that the *shanxiao* reflected shifting frontiers and movements in populations of areas during the 4th century (Han dynasty).

Shen: Shapeshifter that creates illusions. Associated with funerals.

Shu Jing: Tree spirits. Old trees are venerated in China.

Si Xiong: Four Evils. Also known as the Four Fiends, or Four Perils; Hundun (Chaos), Taotie (Gluttony), Taowu (Ignorance) and Qiongqi (Deviousness). These are opposed to the Four Benevolent Animals, Qilin (a Chimera), which even though it looks ferocious only punishes the wicked, Dragon, Turtle and Fenghuang (a composite of various birds).

Taotie, or **Pao Xiao**, has a human face, goat's body, tiger's teeth and eyes near its armpits. It eats humans, luring its victims by crying like an infant. Elizabeth Childs-Johnson in *The Ghost Head Mask and Metamorphic Shang Imagery* defines *taotie* as 'demon devourer' and says it was used to describe Shang ritual art imagery (3rd century BCE). She contends the image was one of metamorphic power, of access to ancestors.

Taowu also has a human face, tiger's and/or pig's feet and an 18 feet-long tail. It can see the past and future, is very fierce and perhaps through these attributes has become identified with history itself (see *The Monster That Is History* by David Der-Wei Wang).

Qionqi looks like a winged tiger. It eats humans from the head down and causes confusion and war.

Hundun is a faceless being representing primordial chaos. The *Chuangtzu* has this famous (and I think very amusing, although that may just be my sense of humour) story:

> The Emperor of the South Sea was called Shu. The Emperor of the North Sea was called Hu. The Emperor of the Centre Sea was called Huntun. From time to time, Hu and Shu met in the centre, and Huntun was very generous to them. They wondered how they could repay his kindness. 'All men have seven openings,' they agreed, 'so that they can eat, hear, breathe, see and so forth. Let's give him some holes!' So every day, they bored a hole into Huntun. On the seventh day, he died.

Hundun: Hole-free Chaos

Another of his stories concerns 'the arts of Mr. Chaos' (*Hundun Shi zhi shu*), in which Confucius denigrates a Taoist sage for his practices. A sack filled with blood representing Hundun was once hung from a tree and shot at with arrows, ritually releasing the lifeblood of Chaos.

Tu Wei Ba Li Hei: Black dragon without a tail that banishes floods.

Wangliang: Once the name of a specific demon, but is now used in a general sense for ghosts and demons. The earliest source mentioning *wangliang* is the 5th to 4th century BCE *Guoyo* (*Discourses of the State*). Xu Shen's *Shuowen jiezi* (121 CE) describes *wangliang* as appearing like a three-year-old child, with red-black colouring, red eyes, long ears and beautiful hair. Ge Hong's *Baopuzi* (c.320 CE) also has this description, as does Gan Bao's *Shoushenji* (c.350 CE), although the latter adds long arms with red claws. *Wangliang* can be demons of rivers and marshes; *chimei* are generally demons of mountains and forests. *Chimeiwangliang* is also used: mountain and water demons, monsters and spirits. Derivatives are *wangxiang* and *fangliang* as water demon and graveyard demon respectively. As variants of a single designation the attributions may vary.

Wu Tou Gui: Headless Ghost. Spirit of those who were killed by decapitation. Wander aimlessly, may approach people to ask where their head is. How they speak without a head is one question, although in some depictions they carry their head by their side. In which case, the second question is why they would need to ask where their head is. Logic however does not need to enter here.

Wu zhi qi: Water demon. Ape-like, with a white head and green body. Was chained up by Yu when he tamed the Great Flood.

Xiao: One-footed mountain demon. Attacks at night.

Yaogui, **Yaomo** or **Yaojing**: Malevolent animal spirits or fallen celestials. *Yaojing* are 'sprites' such as fox spirits.

Ye Cha: Hordes of protector deities that devour ghosts and demons.

You Hun Ye Gui: 'Wandering Souls and Wild Ghosts', active during the Ghost Festival in the 7th Lunar month. Include vengeful ghosts, hungry ghosts and playful ones. They may have no relatives or resting place, or have lost their way (*You Ying Gong*, 'Lost Spirits'). *Gu Hun Ye Gui*, lonely souls and wild ghosts, is a term used to describe homeless and destitute people.

Yu: A fever demon, in the form of a three-legged poisonous malaria-causing turtle.

Yuan Gui: A ghost with a grievance. Restless spirits who cannot be reincarnated. Belief in such can be found in the *Zuo zhuan* (by Zuo Qiuming, a narrative history of the late 4th Century BCE).

Zhong Kui: Due to his ugly appearance, Zhong Kui's achievement in gaining top honours in the Imperial Exams was stripped from him by the Emperor. In anger, Zhong Kui took his own life by hurtling himself headfirst against the palace gates. Yama, the King of Hell, saw potential in him and gave him the title King of Ghosts; he is popularly known as the Demon Queller, his task being to hunt down and keep order among ghosts.

Zhou You Ling: Souls of the drowned, said to be active in particular at a beach called the Weeping Ghost in Hainan. Appearing on the crest of waves, they warn of danger. Shui Gui, Water Ghosts, on the other hand lurk in places where they drowned, drag their victims underwater and take possession of their bodies. The victim's spirit then takes the place of the *shui gui*, and so the cycle continues.

A modern account of apparent encounters with both a fox-spirit and a hungry ghost are given by Stuart Alve Olson in his book *The Jade Emperor's Mind Seal Classic* (pp. 79 to 83), in relation to Ko Hung's writings on ghosts and spirits.

The Three Corpse Demons
(The scrolls they are holding are presumably their reports on the host's
misdeeds).

There are warnings throughout Taoist literature about eating grain which appear congruent with Biblical admonitions such as 'In the sweat of thy face shalt thou eat bread'. The Fall seems to be associated with the rise of agriculture, with wheat as the Forbidden Fruit.

'... the people of mysterious antiquity, they reached old age because they remained in leisure and never ate any grains.' (From the *Most High Numinous Treasure*. The term *lingbao*, or Numinous Treasure, described an object or medium (*bao*) inhabited by a spirit (*ling*). The scriptures using the name helped shape Taoist thought and are first dated to c. 400 CE, although may be earlier).

The hard labour of tilling the land and relying on crops that succeeded the era of foraging and hunting was an existence vulnerable to the elements and natural disasters. Famine is a recurrent tragedy in Chinese history. The Agricultural Revolution that began some 10,000 years ago made life generally more difficult than that of hunting-gathering, with its resultant population explosion, poorer diet and tying people to the land. It was not the great progressive evolutionary leap it has been thought to be. Some of the ancient deities in a variety of cultures are interestingly gods of both death and grain: Osiris and Gwyn ap Nudd as two to begin with.

The cereals are the *wu ku* or Five Grains: rice, oats, millet, wheat and soya. These fed the Three Worms, or Corpse Demons, (i.e. corpse-inducing demons) who reported any bad conduct by the host to the Celestial Bureaucracy, which accordingly took away time from the subject's lifespan; the Worm's aim was to shorten their host's life in order to themselves evolve. The Worms may of course have been observed as actual intestinal parasites.

Ge Hong lists five corpse-demons in *Prescriptions Within Arm's Reach for Use in Emergencies*: Flying corpses that bore through the skin into the inner organs; Wind corpses caused by windy weather; Reclusive corpses which make themselves known when there is a sound of crying, or at funerals; Sinking corpses that cause pain in the organs when cold; and finally, Corpse infestation, the cause of major ill health.

The seven *p'o*, another group of inner demons, are poetically named as Hidden Dung, Sparrow-Sex, Corpse Dog, Flying Venom, Rot Lung, Greedy Guts, and Filth for Removal. To add further complexity, an addition of nine worms incite the victim to evil deeds.

Bigu is the dietary practice of refraining from eating grains. The cult of the Stove God is also involved here, and by extension the alchemists' references to the 'Inner Furnace' and 'Cauldrons'. There is an extensive study of the subject by Dannaway (*Yoked to Earth*: see bibliography) who includes an invaluable comparison to our current wave of food intolerance, with gluten clinically linked to Coeliac disease, schizophrenia, diabetes and cancer. As he notes, Taoists have for centuries alleged that eating grain actually increases hunger, and recent research confirms this. The Taoist adept carefully scrutinised the effect of diet long before it became a contemporary medical concern. Soya, the staple 'Health Food', is also reportedly highly damaging, and linked to the development of Alzheimer's amongst other conditions.

ENTITIES OF THE TAO

'One does not become enlightened by imagining figures of the
light, but by making the darkness conscious.' Jung.

ALTHOUGH SOME prefer to interpret Taoism purely as a philosophy,
the religious-magical aspect is certainly not an anachronism, with a
direct history in teaching right down to the present day, and three
major sects involved in magical practice, the *Mao-shan*, *Kunlun*, and
Tianshi (Celestial Teachers).

The 'current' of Chinese magic naturally evokes a China of the
imagination, a thought or feeling that can bear little resemblance to
the 'real', that is, the country now facing increased commercialisation
and industrial pollution. The art nevertheless holds its own vitality,
and has been finding at least some transference and integration into
Western culture with the relative permeability of communication
boundaries. Kuan Yin, the deity associated with compassion (see *Kuan
Yin in the West: Invocation and Evocation*) has notably been eagerly adopted
through the impact of both Buddhism and Feminism, although as
with any adaptation of foreign cultural icons there is the danger of
taking the core energy of the image out of context.

Chinese shamanism, or *wuism*, comes from ancient Neolithic
cultures, such as the Hongshan. A *wu* (shaman) could be either male
or female. In the early Shang dynasty, the Cosmos dominated nature,
and contact with the divine was made by shamanic dance or trance,
or the rational use of the bone oracle. Later in a more agrarian phase,
during the Zhou era, Nature dominated. *Tian* and *Di*, Heaven and
Earth, formed a complimentary duality. The *tao-shih* or Taoist priest
is also known as a *yu-jen*, 'feather man'; flying immortals had coats
of feathers, and on achieving immortality the *tao-shih* were supposed
to ascend to heaven in plain view, hence 'feather men'. It is an
archetypal shamanic form of attire. The Han folk religion venerates
the forces of nature, with harmful influences being exorcised. The
Yao ethnic religion is defined as Yao Taoism, as every male adult in

Yao society is initiated as a Taoist. As a death rite, the priest purifies
the dead person's body with a water ritual, the *zoux sin*, to remove evil
spirits.

Chinese gods, or as they could be interpreted in a sense patron
saints, are *shen-ming*, 'radiance of the celestial soul'. In a Taoist
magical viewpoint, humans are endowed with many souls and are
conglomerations of differentiated universal energies. Within the body
are *hun*, god-souls, and *p'o*, demon-souls. The latter are related to the
skeleton, and rail against the *hun* authority by aiming to free themselves
and return the bones to earth. Richard Wilhelm in his discussion of
The Secret of the Golden Flower notes the bipolar tension of duality both
within the world and in the individual, and describes the interaction
of *hun* and *p'o* as 'the interplay of two psychic structures' (p.14), the
hun being the Yang principle, the *p'o* Yin. He says that '...both contain
in their written form the sign for demon'. *Hun* is constructed of the
characters for 'demon' and 'cloud', and *p'o* of those for 'demon' and
'white'. (Demon here is not construed as evil.) *P'o* also translates as
'lunar brightness', *hun* as soul or spirit. The *hun* transcends the body
at death, the *p'o* remains. The Yin-Yang identification with *p'o* and
hun respectively occurred in the late 4th to early 3rd centuries BCE.
In Wu Xing theory, the *hun* soul corresponds to the liver and blood,
the *p'o* to the lungs and breath. *Sanhunqipo*, 'three *hun* and seven *p'o*',
is another categorisation. The *fangshi* ('occult prescription specialists'
or magicians) could summon the *hun* and *p'o* back into a deceased
person's body. Alchemical pills might be used as well as the *fu* (recall)
ritual.

Seal Script for Hun   Seal Script for P'o

There are also the three 'corpses' or 'corpse worms' within the body which can cause illness and even encourage demons to enter. As noted before, the dietary advice of avoiding grains was aimed at starving these worms.

The word *Shen* can be interpreted both as deities (36,000 of which inhabit both the universe and also the body of each human) and as the personal spirit, being one of the Three Treasures; the other two are Essence (*Ching*) and Primordial Energy (*Yuan Chi*). There is a further definition of *Shen* as states of mind: ordinary consciousness or *shih-shen* and spiritual consciousness, *yuan-shen*. *Shen* (heavenly Yang) spirits have a counterpart in the *kuei*, ghosts or demons, given a Yin attribution.

There are three views of the body in Chinese spirituality: theological, tied to the notion of divine energies; empirical, originating practices of Chinese medicine; and the vision of the body as a symbolic country, where exists mountains, lakes and courtyards along with their inhabitants. The Queen of the West is an example of one of these, also identified as the Mother and the Wife, the feminine aspect of Tao reigning in the abdomen's ocean sphere as an internal deity. As Kristofer Schipper has said, 'the true Taoist pantheon exists within us, created by our vital energies.' And, 'The Taoist carries his gods within himself.' (*The Taoist Body*).

As I made the point in 'A General Perspective of the Demonic', a principle difference between Western and Taoist approaches to spiritual/magical contact with non-human entities is that the Taoist realises such communion through the body and not exclusively as 'out there'. One class of entity, as illustration, is associated with the spine – an internal realisation rather than external. This could be seen as the formation of a depth psychology although it was not framed in the recognisable terms of psychoanalysis but by metaphors of outer alchemy. Incidentally, Isa Gucciardi's *Depth Hypnosis* has a value in communing with 'darkside' intelligences, but we are ranging outside of our immediate scope there.

What was seen as the negative influence of external gods of the common people, false gods and therefore demons, could be neutralised by the Taoist who converted their energies in his own body. This form of exorcism was accomplished covertly and relates to the 'Way of Demons' taught by Chang Tao-ling, who is attributed by some as being the true founder of Taoism.

The Celestial Teachers, or Celestial Masters sect dates back to Chang's revelations in 142 CE. Under Emperor Wu (140-86 BCE) Confucianism had become the state doctrine although regional belief and administration differed. Communes were organized and led by ordained masters, somewhat like the democratic states of ancient Greece. As happened in other cultures with other religions, local deities were demonised by Taoism as a way of distinguishing itself, and these entities were also assimilated into its pantheon to enhance its power.

There was no particular division of entities into good and bad. *Guishen*, 'demons and sundry spirits', ranged from purely evil to judiciously helpful. Early demonography was concerned with charting their nature, and although many of these volumes have been lost there are representative ones that are extant and have been translated. The *Nuqing guilu* or *Demon Statutes of Lady Blue* says, 'If one knows the name of the demon, it will return to its real form and no longer harass one'. The *Nuqing* as a Taoist scripture functions as an aid for followers of the Tao, so ethically if the Taoist acts correctly there is little to fear. The demons' function from this viewpoint is to punish wrongdoing. Later, humans were no longer held to be so responsible for their own misfortune, and blame was ascribed to demonic action, so the Taoist moral code was circumvented by this point.

EXORCISM

'She was in the night again, and the doll was herself.' Angela Carter, *The Magic Toyshop*.

DEMONS ARE not always personalised. Those that aren't are perhaps the worst kind. The ones with identities can be exorcised; that which can be named can be controlled. However, the ambiguous are less easily ordered.

The Jesuits made records of Taoist methods of exorcism during the late Ming period, which were quite theatrical in comparison to their own methods of dispersing holy water and praying; Taoist priests used incantations but also shouted to get rid of malevolent entities, and employed demonic illustrations in ink on yellow paper. Members of the *fashi* (religious ceremony or ritual) perform exorcisms on individuals either possessed or haunted by spirits, or to drive away spirits from a location as part of a festival. The procedures involve chanting, prayer and particular physical gestures and movement.

Evil spirits are believed to only be able to move in straight lines, hence the circular or swirling movement in physical banishment rituals such as the circle, or in the brush strokes used to dispel them in writing talismans. Malevolent nature spirits include Forest, Mountain, Water and Ground demons, with the latter connected to cemeteries.

The Nuo folk religion is connected to the Tujia people and as an exorcistic movement had influence on Taoism. 'Xiang' can be interpreted as 'image' or 'vision', so the *fangxiangshi* is 'Master of images', or 'Master who assists the astral square'. The *fangxiangshi*, ritual exorcist leads the Nuo ritual, clearing demons from dwellings and keeping *wangliang* spirits away from burial chambers during funeral processions so that the corpse is not eaten. The *Da* (Great) *Nuo* ceremony has been associated with Zhong Kui cults. The *Da Yu* was a Great Exorcism Rite, performed formally; *Yu* were purification rites held spontaneously to counteract the curses of ancestor spirits.

The *fang* attribution is commonly interpreted as *sifang* or 'four directions', and is therefore an idea of orientation or locality. Boltz (*A Survey of Taoist Literature, 10th to 17th Centuries*) has made the suggestion along with other scholars that, given the similarity between the names *fangxiangshi* and the *fangliang, wangliang* and *wangxiang* demons, there is an identification or personification between them – the exorcist exorcises himself. An adjunct to this is the practice also known in other traditions of absorbing the demon into oneself, a highly advanced and dangerous procedure due to the possibility of possession. Being possessed purposely is strongly advised against as causing a negative reaction in the body.

Originating in the Eastern Zhou (771-256 BCE), *fangxiangshi* were employed during the Han dynasty (206-220 CE) and continue their employment privately in the present day. Traditionally a bearskin with four gold eyes, to see in the four directions, and a ghost head or demon mask (*guitou*) is worn. Wearing a bear skin transformed the exorcist into that creature in order to dispel ghosts and evil. Shamanism, as mediating between the human and spirit worlds, required metamorphosis from human to animal to grant access to the realm of spirits. Also worn were 'black coats and red skirts' (*Book of the Later Han*, 5th Century).

Spirits can be Yang by nature (good) or Yin (evil). Ghosts need energy to manifest in appearance, either a human presence or environmental energy such as light. Demons, existing in the Yin energetic realms, manifest in darkness, absorbing life energy and causing fear and paralysis. Establishing a personal relationship with the divine, however formulated, can help to protect.

Both the Stabbing Demon (*tz'u kuei*) and Wolf Demon (*lang kuei*) are dealt with by firing jujube arrows at them from a peach bow ('exorcistic archery'). A Whirlwind Demon (*p'iao feng*) can be dispatched by throwing a shoe at it. Other things that can be effective in dispelling demons when thrown at them include white stones and excrement. An almanac discovered at Shuihudi recommends pellets of dog crap be thrown at demonic spirits to repel them. Animals can turn into demons upon death if they were mistreated in life.

Peachwood is a ubiquitous protective material. Shouting 'No' is an exorcistic expletive in either English or Chinese. Apart from formal ritual banishing which can include shouting, beating a drum and bell-ringing, running water repels demons, and attacks can be offset by doing the unexpected.

External anomalies can be attributed to human states of being. Yi Feng (c. 1st century BCE) believed such irregularities were caused by *qi* obstruction; when it counter-flowed it caused 'motion' in heaven and earth. Psychological states such as emotional disturbance can create psychic forms of malaise, known as Qi Deviations. A posture for counteracting this is the 'Closed Circuit'; sitting, elbows resting on knees, the soles of the feet placed together and the hands held in a prayer form. Also there are treatments under the discipline of Medical Qi Gong. Other physical postures recommended in the *Shui-hu-ti* manuscripts include 'the winnowing basket' and the 'leaning stance' (it is not explained how these are performed) and sleeping on one's side with knees bent, which is said to increase *qi* and protect against demons.

Puppet theatre troupes could be called to exorcise evil influences including demons. Marionettes are consecrated and represent universal energy. The stage is a sacred area with an altar, and talismans are written in the four corners. The puppeteer carries a fifth, the central one. There are 36 bodies with 72 heads, making the magical number 108. The most powerful of the puppets are (of course) the clowns.

CHE-SOAH

In 1976 John McCreery recorded a rite called *che ngo-kui* ('controlling/propitiating the Five Ghosts') performed by a Taoist healer in Taipei. Ong Kok-hui, who claimed to be a 'Red-Head Master of Magic' of the Heavenly Master sect, had founded a temple to the goddess Ma-cho. Even if his qualification is not definitely established, the exorcistic rite described is an interesting one. Ong used a divination technique, *bi-koa*; the client was asked to pray to Ma-cho as Ong circled the end of a writing brush in a dish of uncooked rice while reciting an incantation. The client took two pinches of rice from the centre of the plate and from these Ong removed eight grains at a time until eight or fewer were left. The result was a pair of numbers indicating one of the I Ching's hexagrams. He then looked up in a notebook the names of demons associated with the hexagram.

Once having identified the demons, the rite to deal with them was performed (*che-soah*, 'controlling/propitiating demons'). The client lit three sticks of incense and stood in the street facing the opposite direction of the temple, praying to the demons and vowing appropriate offerings would be made. Images of the demons and a *the-sin*, 'substitute', acting as a scapegoat for the client, were placed in baskets. These were then put outside the temple until it was confirmed the demons had accepted the offerings, at which point they were brought inside for final exorcism.

The exorcist's attitude was deferential to the gods invoked and superior to the demons. Holding three sticks of incense in each hand, the burning tips were inclined toward the demon images but away from the gods while he performed gestures and made invocations. Once the demons were driven away, the images and substitute were passed over the client's body, and in conclusion the client stepped over seven sheets of burning spirit money.

Paper dolls represented the demons, human in form but with horns and fur kilts (see cover image). The substitute was a rice straw doll dressed in one of the client's shirts, and the offerings were food and spirit money. There were five parts to the ritual: addressing the demons, invoking the gods, consecration of the *the-sin*, divining of the demon's response and pronouncing the exorcism complete. In finding the answer, divining blocks were used, wooden crescents round on one side and flat on the other. If falling with one round and one flat side up, it indicated that Yin and Yang were balanced, a favourable reply. If a negative response, more spirit money could be offered or the demons invited to leave from a different direction than east. In the final exorcism, the demons were conflated with the substitute.

The Demon Drugs

Hallucinogenic plants were studied and categorised in texts such as the *Shennon Bencaojing* of c. 200- 250 CE. These included those used to communicate with spirits: *Langdang* (Hyoscamus niger), the seeds of which were treated by soaking in vinegar and milk; *Shanglu* (Phytolacca acinosa, or Pokeweed), the root of which (one with the red root, the other type is white) was used for summoning spirits, but is very poisonous; *Yunshi* (Caesalpinia decapetala), which if burned could be used to summon spirits, or to exorcise them; and *Dema* (Cannabis sativa), which has been used in China since the Neolithic age. The female plants (*ju*) produce more cannabinoids. To enable spirit communication the buds were ingested over a long time. As recorded in the *Wushang Biyao*, a Taoist encyclopedia of circa 570 CE, cannabis was added to ritual incense burners. From the *Wu Tsang Ching* (6th C.) it is said, 'If you wish to command the appearance of demonic apparitions, consume constantly the flowers of the hemp plant.'

By ingesting an elixir as detailed in *The Book of the Nine Elixirs* (*Huangdi jiuding shendan jingjue*), 'Gods and Demons will become your attendants and offer protection.'[4] Other prescriptions include:

'If you smear the eyes of a person or the walls of a city with the Reverted Elixir, the hundred demons will flee.'

'If you keep in your hand one pill of the Fixed Elixir, the size of a date stone, the hundred demons will be exterminated.'

'Marking the doors with the Fixed Elixir, the hundred calamities, the myriad spirits, and the *chimei* and *wangliang* demons will dare not come before you.'

The method for making the Pellet for Expelling Demons is detailed in the *Book of Great Clarity* (*Taiqing jing tianshi koujue*), translated by Pregadio, op. cit. Equal quantities of 17 ingredients are pounded, sieved and mixed with the juice of anise follicles and formed into pellets the size of a hen's egg yolk. These are cinnabar, realgar, orpiment, tortoise shell, black veratrum root, peach pits, aconite tuber collected in autumn, great bulb of pinellia tuberifera, poison ivy, sulphur, croton seed, rhinoceros horn, umbrella leaf, musk, spindle tree wings and dried centipedes. The pellets are burnt to effect exorcism.

As a tangential note, black or adverse magic came under the name *Gu* (poison). Venomous creatures would be sealed together in a container, the one survivor having absorbed the others' toxins. It would be transformed into a demon/spirit and used for harmful purposes, the poison from the creature being placed in the victim's food or drink and causing hallucinations as well as physical detriment. *Gu* sorcerers were traditionally beheaded and their heads placed on pikes.

---

4   See Pregadio, *Great Clarity: Daoism and Alchemy in Early Medieval China.*

Cults and Demons

Lurid headlines about 'The Chinese Cult that Kills Demons' or 'China's Demon-Killing Cult' turned out to be an isolated incident in a Shandong McDonalds in 2014, when a woman was killed by members of 'The Church of Almighty God', which claims Jesus was resurrected in China as a female. It seems the victim refused to give her phone number to them and was attacked for being an 'evil spirit'. 'She was a demon. We had to destroy her,' said one of the murderers, Zhang Lidong. He and his daughter Zhang Fan were executed.

Beating a human being to death in order to exorcise or destroy a non-human creature is an extreme measure whichever way one looks at it. Whether the poor lady was perceived purely as a demon, like some kind of hallucination, or as a possessing entity, either way the demonic was here seen as *any innocent passerby* outside the 'sane' circle of the group. The Church of Almighty God has also condemned the Chinese government itself as the 'Red Dragon' (it's unknown if it has appropriated any Blakean mysticism in that rendering).

Naturally, the State is clamping down on the Church.

Magician and Fox-Spirit
From 'The Dragon, Image and Demon'

Demon Legislation

'The Menu is Not the Meal.' Alan Watts.

Naming is used to make something real through identification. The Unknown is commonly an anomaly; the adept knows the realm of the invisible through names, and takes control in such manner, just as Confucian administrative order was kept by its application of titles. Knowledge of names as empowerment was a prominent feature of the Warring States period.

Knowing the true names of demons is a way of controlling them, as in the *Nuqing guilu*, the *Demon Statutes of Lady Blue*, of putting them back in their proper place and restoring the order of cosmic law. Dating from the late 3rd century CE, the *Nuqing guilu* is said to be the earliest surviving Taoist scripture. It records the names of quasi-demons who can be made to serve the Taoist priest.

Nature spirits, divinised humans, and high gods of the state which were identified as demons and had a chaotic effect on the world could also be exorcised by overt Taoist ritual, an empowering action. In Magical Taoism, two kinds of power are recognised: that coming from nature, and that from spirits and deities. Taoist practitioners tend to use both.

The Demon Statutes promised control over spirits through knowledge of their names and forms. They were supposedly sent down from The Great Tao in eight scrolls. This was a pivotal time when the Taoists rejected sacrifice as a propitiatory action and took hold of a new consciousness, a personal control over nature.

'The Most High Great Tao... At the noon hour on the seventh day of the seventh month... sent down these Demon Statutes in eight scrolls, recording the names and surnames of the Spirits of the Realm...

'He charged the Celestial Master with it, causing him to command the Spirits... Since then, when men or women of the Tao see my secret scripture and know the surnames and names of demons..., myriad demons will not interfere with them, and the thousand gods will submit to them.' (See Kleeman, 'Exorcizing the Six Heavens: The Role of Traditional State Deities in the Demon Statutes of Lady Blue,' in *Exorcism in Religious Daoism: A Berlin Symposium*, 2011).

As the First Heavenly Master, Chang received the One energy, that is, the presence of Lao Tzu, the First Being from Original Chaos. He made a covenant with the forces of the old order and began a new world, that of the Great Peace (*t'ai-p'ing*), involving a new cosmology of the gods of the Orthodox One. Adepts of the Orthodox One community received a *fu* symbol, which became a protective force and assumed a human form that the adept learnt to see and to activate its influence. This essence, known as the Agent, also had a number of other projections, listed as a register (*lu*).

By the time the adept was old enough to marry, the register would number 75 protective gods. Marriage united the couple's energies to a total of 150 gods, but the same powers also controlled the adept's conduct. Exclusion from the system meant a fall into the sphere of 'dead energies' of the Six Heavens.

The term Six Heavens was directed at the world of profane religion rejected by the Taoists. Thus demons are as noted identified with state cult deities, such as the 'Ten Thousand Foot Demon of High Heaven' being the demonic form of the state's 'Supreme Thearch of Lofty Heaven'.

The Demon Statutes states, 'The current age is benighted, evil and disordered. There are no perfected deities to be seen, only demons who trouble humans.' Knowledge of the names of the six palaces in the centre of the Six Heavens brings power over the demonic forces.

Deities were of an ambiguous nature; household gods, primarily protective, such as the gods of the hearth, the door and the well, are listed as demons in the Statutes, according to which the gods of the gate and door are gods by day and demons at night. ('... the sire of the Gate and the Attendant of the Door. During the day they are gods who bless the home; at night they become demons'). Lady

Blue is the interpretation of *nuqing*, also rendered as *nvqing*. The ideogram of *qing* derives from an image of sprouting plant life, hence Wood and nature. In the Chinese Five Element theory (*Wu Hsing*), within the Wood element the Azure Dragon or Qinglong is one of the four Constellation symbols and represents the east and spring. Also associated is the planet Jupiter, another blue correspondence familiar in Western symbolism. There is not a single definition for blue in Chinese; *qing* is translated as green, blue or black. Perhaps we could propose here a purposeful dualism in interpretation, with blue-green representing growth and birth, while blue-black can be symbolic of realms of involution and death. According to one of many explanations of the idea of Three Worlds, the Tao transmitted subtle energies of three colours: the Obscure, Primordial and Initial Energies. The Obscure is blue-black and Heaven; the Initial is yellow and Earth; the Primordial is white and Tao.

With this perceptual merging of colour, which may be dependent on the pictorial basis of Chinese language, can be read a number of spiritual attributions: the blue of Heaven or blue-black Obscure. The Chinese blue being ever-shifting and indistinct becomes associated with the dead; in Chinese funerals the body of the deceased is covered with a light-blue cloth.

There is practically nothing said about Lady Blue in the text of *The Demon Statutes* with which she is associated, although she is also credited with an 'imperial edict' (*zhaoshu*) cited often in medieval grave documents. She is not a historical figure, though she is possibly an ancient demiurge such as Nuwa, who repaired heaven.

She is linked with the world of the dead and the hells. Additionally, from the colour blue we can assume the connection with an influence in the realm of the dead; the feminine attribution we could reflect has something important to say when the society of the time was governed by a patriarchal and repressive state Confucianism. Conversely there was a tradition of respect and veneration toward women within Taoism. The Immortal Sisters was the name given to female Taoist adepts; it was said that 'The body of the Tao is a woman' (see Schipper), and an essential symbol was 'The Mysterious Female'. Moreover, the Taoist feminine was a way of thinking, a mode of consciousness. Male Taoists adopted a female attitude to the extent of squatting instead of standing when urinating.

Lady Blue is then an abstract linguistic symbol, a state of mind, and a very ancient deity. Ideas come into consciousness at a particular moment that is cogently appropriate for that time. The concept of Lady Blue as feminine mode of energy related to the control of demons is emblematic of the clearing of old thought, the old form of government. There is therefore a political motivation as Taoism established itself through the Celestial Teachers by the demonising of the old order's gods.

At the same time *The Statutes* were an ordered way of reconstituting thought – an internal exorcism process. The conjuration or invoking of Lady Blue is an outer manifestation of a collective process that makes sense of and coheres the multiple forces of dissolution, being that the Priest or adept is now seen as controller of the universal energies. The Lady arises from the Obscure, or the Underworld, the labyrinthine land of the dead and the deep layers below initial and primordial realms, or below our conscious level.

Those Oriental female deities that are now becoming more consciously appreciated in the West as evocative of sexual equality globally are perhaps representative of the three classic Chinese worlds. Kuan Yin is very important as a 'bridge' deity, helping us to both cross the cultural divide and enabling our own individual evolution. Her embodiment of compassion manifests to offset the sensory deferment that is now occurring through an increasing dislocation of The Human by technology.

Tsi Ku is known as The Purple Lady. She seeks to appear at the Initial or earth level. She presides over arts of divination such as Spirit Writing, providing a medium between earth and the Other dimensions, and possesses the women of households at New Year. In the respect of an earth entity she is also associated with the outhouse as The Lady of the Privy, a symbol of dense earthiness. Her appearance is of having a stunningly beautiful upper body while her lower half is smoke.

The earthiness of toilet deities is representative of human base functions being 'holy after another manner'. There are several Japanese toilet deities such as Toire no Hanako-san, Aka-Manto, Akaname, Kashima Reiko and Kawaya no-kami, as well as the Babylonian Sulak, the demon Belphegor and the Roman Crepitus, Cloacina the sewer goddess, and Stercutius the god of dung. As any care worker will tell you, toward the end of a round of earthly existence, it's all about evacuation.

The third entity acting as signifier of the Worlds is Lady Blue from the sphere of the Obscure. Her manifestation symbolises a radical change in the political sphere and a shift in thought as we achieve a new level of understanding individually and collectively. It could be said that her mission in being called into activity now is once more the eradication of demons, those of our own age and culture, which include political deifications of Mammon and the technocracy. The Dead Energies are in our own time electronic frequencies.

Because, it has been said, you do not necessarily choose deities so much as they may choose you, there is a 'mutual arising' (*hsiang sheng*) or as the Buddhist term has it, 'dependent co-origination' where contact is established, to coin a phrase, 'out of the blue'. Tradition has it that connection to higher spiritual understanding requires corresponding inner qualities in the seeker, and so at a certain time without apparent focus on result appears the Being. In relation the full knowledge and conversation of an entity such as Lady Blue is hidden at the core of an essential paradigm shift. She is, as the translation of her name implies, the 'Mysterious Female' of the Tao, a blank slate without image or qualities, yet immediately there 'mutually arises' a form from nothingness.

A note of caution has been sounded by one popular writer on Taoism, Eva Wong. She has written, 'Magical Taoism is not a path that you can dabble with and then abandon.' It requires commitment and a teacher familiar with the system.

She describes how in order to cultivate vital energy the body is divided into three parts, upper, middle and lower, with each part guarded by eight Jing deities. Heaven = Universal Spiritual laws. The Kingdom = The Body. The colour Yellow refers to the Earth element central to the Five Elements, surrounded by the rest of them (The Court).

I have come across a reference to there being eight demons inhabiting the brain which unfortunately now eludes me, possibly due to the demon governing memory. Timothy Leary's eight-circuit brain theory, developed by Robert Anton Wilson, could be appended for further research.

Part of a Song dynasty stone rubbing of Wang Xizhi's manuscript (356
CE) of the *Huang Ting Jing* or *Yellow Court Classic*, a Taoist Alchemical
meditation text dated to 288 CE. The attributed author is Wei Huacun
(265-317), a founder of the Shangqing (Highest Purity) tradition.

Ritual

'And how then...shall I reconcile this Art Magick with that Way of the Tao which achieveth all Things by doing Nothing? But this have I already declared to thee in Part, shewing that thou canst do no magick save it be thy Nature to do Magick, and so the true Nothing for thee.' (Crowley, 'On the Necessity of the Will', *Liber Aleph*).

CONSIDERING THE mechanics of Taoist ritual and the role of shadow and opposition in it, most accounts focus purely on the outward display and have no account of the inner workings. By far the larger part of the ritual takes place 'off stage' in the imagining of the practitioner/s and the extradimensional worlds of Tao. The performance thereby opposes the category of The Natural by beckoning the supranatural and scattering the shadow force of materiality, switching values between the substantial and insubstantial.

Despite the inclination to draw comparisons through the apparent similarities in ritual tools and operation, as we will see further on, we should be wary of assuming the Taoist ritualist works in a manner conducive to Western magic in any potentially syncretic manner. The apparition rather than the apparent is the energy in motion here.

Following the device of Inversion, it's not a case of summoning demons, which is a bit presumptuous; they more likely summon you if they need you for a certain creative task, say, such as writing a book on demons.

The approaches to magic have classically been biased toward either pure intellect (High Ritualism) or to physical expression (Shamanic Dance). The origin of Chinese ritual magic is accredited to the Yellow Emperor, Huang Di (c. 2697 – 2597 BCE). Later, shamanic sorcery was used in harnessing the power of star gods, indicating an interest in the constellations. The first Taoist magical rituals probably date to the Qin and early Han period (221 BCE to 24 CE).

As in the West, there are categorisations of low or sympathetic magic and high ritual magic, the aim of which is usually to contact entities. Also similar are the divisions into Black, White and Grey magic depending on whether one is working for selfish or altruistic reasons, although there is the argument that there is no 'grey' magic, you either work with good or evil. The power for working magic is not the same as Qi; it is a different form and more concentrated. Evil sorcery is that which requires a sacrifice; people are attracted to it as it offers relatively quick results, but the ultimate result is not worth it.

Sorcery employs such familiar techniques as using wax or paper dolls with hair or nail clippings from an intended target attached in order to create a psychic link, or using blood or other bodily fluids, and the use of talismans and spells. Using magic for evil purposes eventually destroys the sorcerer – that is a rule of esoteric law.

With ritual, the Taoist is immersed in the Source, the sacred manifestation of multiple worlds and beings. There are complex purification and offering rites requiring priests who have trained for years, and liturgical scriptures chanted in monastic communities, but one can also perform individual ritual before a personal altar.

Ritual is designed to periodically dissociate us from our daily involvement in worldly affairs, with paraphernalia used to impress upon the mind a sense of entering the noumenal through a gateway. In one way then, ideally, we do not need such trickery. The earthy nature of Taoism exemplified by the teachings of such sages as Chuang-tzu can be interpreted as implying our native immersion within the Tao, through all that is around us. Ritual therefore is a form of play; indeed, puppet theatre is used by Taoist masters for sacred performances as we have seen.

Within the folk religion outside of official Taoism, Folk Taoism exists with *Daoshi* ('masters of the Tao') and *fashi* ('masters of rites', the 'red hat' priests) marrying and performing rituals for communities or privately. *Zhengyi daoshi* ('black hat' priests) emphasise their Taoist tradition. The main rituals are for Purification, Offering or Invocation, Funerals and Exorcism.

Primarily the practitioner undergoes internal training such as the ability to visualise rising to Heaven to meet the gods. Focus of attention is intensified by the accoutrements of ritual. Ceremonial clothing also ritually distances the subject from the mundane world. There are different classes of robe, including for casual use, for ceremony and ritual, of different colours and material, cotton, linen or silk, of various designs and with a number of appropriately symbolic patterns on them.

A Taoist priest's hat represents the anointing of Heaven, and cloth-soled shoes are worn. As a belt, a red rope is worn around the magician's waist representing containment of the *Ling Shen* or Magical Spirit as well as protection. It can be placed on the ground if required as a magic circle surrounding the practitioner.

For a personal altar, a deity may be selected according to individual concerns. The altar table represents the world of matter beneath light. There are two altars, the Earth altar and the Central altar behind it, representing the celestial realm. Two candles symbolizing sun and moon, Yang and Yin, or the eyes, are lit to open proceedings, there also being an altar bell to mark three rounds of bowing or prostration.

The altar incense burner is a focal point in ceremonies, with its smoke infusing the ritual space and the body of the officiant with sacred energy. It purifies the temple and draws deities. The Incense Burner acquired a sacred focus in ancient China as an object of veneration in itself. Temple burners are placed outside the altar, in the courtyard. Altar burners are placed on the Earth altar. Incense is placed in the burner with the left hand. Incense is used for worship, purification or protection, and has three basic functions: to purify the space around the altar, alert deities a ritual is taking place, and to draw them to the altar.

Three sticks of incense are also lit, which represent the *Jing*, *Qi* and *Shen* of the body: essence, energy and spirit. These relate alchemically to Salt, Mercury and Sulfur respectively. There is an hallucinogenic aspect to the smoke which comes into play for divination and communing with spirits. Various ingredients are used for incense according to requirements. Smoke rises, ashes fall, symbolic of spirit rising above the material world and into the *Wuji*, the realm of the infinite. Burned in front of objects representing the force or deity one wishes to communicate with, incense smoke is used as a medium to carry the intent to that power. The light of the sticks has its own purpose of keeping demons away.

Incense should not be blown onto to extinguish it or increase the smoke. Instead it is fanned. There are various customs held on the burning of incense sticks and the offerings or vows made in accompaniment. Ashes have their own power and can be mixed with chicken blood to write talismans.

A wooden rice container or earthenware jars are used to contain spirits, although 'containing' spirits is a controversial area. An altar cup is used to hold holy water, traditionally from a well, ocean, lake, river or rain. River water is used for exorcisms. Wine may also sometimes be used, and blood and wine mixed together.

The magical sword summons or dispels spirits. It can be made of peachwood, the peach being a symbol of immortality, or of 108 old Chinese coins which should all be of the same Dynasty. Peach wood (*t'ao-fu*) is popularly credited with offering protection against evil spirits.

A Bagua (eight trigram) symbol is often inscribed around the edge of magic mirrors. Other instruments may include a compass for *feng-shui* and to detect the presence of spirits, a flag, staff, spear, whisk, fan, 'report tablet' constructed of copper, magical seal, and a pen to write talismans, which may be offered by being burnt on a ceramic altar dish. The ashes then acquire their own power and may be hidden or perhaps used as energised compost for a particular plant. Talismans are typically written in red ink or blood, or blood mixed with black ink, on a strip of yellow paper. They can also be drawn in the air with smoke or the tip of the wooden sword.

Animal masks are sometimes worn for protective purposes against black magic, and animal totems can be exercised along with such familiar practices of spiritualism as Spirit Possession and Automatic Writing.

Chants, prayers or silent meditation may be used. There is of course an inner and outer aspect to the performance, including hand gestures and forms, or *mudras*. An offering may include 'spirit money' being burnt.

The five altar Gods represent the five elements and directions: North/Water, South/Fire, East/Wood, West/Metal, and Centre/Earth. Each of the elements corresponds, as in Traditional Chinese Medicine (TCM), to a physical organ. Water is associated with the Kidneys, Fire with the Heart, Wood with the Liver, Metal with the Lungs, and Earth with the Spleen. Good fortune comes from the East, the direction the sun rises. Bad fortune or psychic attacks come from the West, where the sun sets. Three bows are made to each direction in opening and closing ceremonies; bowing can also be combined with a secret hand sign. The bow is a form of etiquette, of communicating with the spirit realm by showing respect, and a means of generating energy. Magical vision is an offshoot of training – to actually see spirits or forms of energy. A higher aspect of this is to see things in the Celestial Realm.

There are numerous invocations. The *Huang-t'ing ching*, or *Classic Treatise on the Yellow Castle* (or Court/Hall) is a 3rd century CE work, the recitation of which confers immortality, protection from evil and contact with the inner deities. 'Yellow Castle' refers to the heart (in some texts, to the spleen or pancreas, these organs all being associated in the Five Element theory), and also to the relation between the three centres of Heaven, Earth and Humanity.

Generally then, as applies to either Eastern or Western forms of ritual, and whether we follow an established tradition or a personal spontaneous method, there should be a preparatory stage of clearing a space and ensuring no disturbance, with a protective aspect such as the drawing of a circle around the practitioner. Following this the Call is made to a force or deities, bringing in energy. The supplication for whatever aim is desired is made, and then a banishing, closing of the ritual and the restoration of normal consciousness.

Masks

Chinese shamanic masks are used for funeral rites and exorcisms. There are also festive and theatrical masks. Theatrical ones have a colour symbolism which means the character is immediately read; black represents neutrality or integrity, red is positive virtues, yellow and white are used for cruelty and malevolence, blue for wisdom, gold and silver for spirit beings, whether gods or demons. Green is for impulsive behaviour and violence, purple for justice.

The Nuo drama was designed to drive away evil, and was supposedly begun by the grandson of Huang Di, Zhuan Xiang. Nuo originally meant a pattern step to disperse evil, and it has also been interpreted as the sound made by the exorcist scaring away demons. The masks were made of camphor or willow; it is held that these woods contain spirits. Performance of the drama evolved into dance.

In Yunnan, Nuo drama consists of dancers body-painted as leopards. The dance is still designed to drive away devils.

Bian Lian, 'face-changing', is a part of Sichuan opera, a secretive artform involving the rapid changing of masks or other methods of altering the appearance, including blowing dust or dragging greasepaint across the face.

Chinese Demon Mask, from Beijing.

Nuo Ritual Demon Mask.

Bugang, Yubu, and Bagua Circle Walking

'If one aspires to reach the Tao, one should practice walking in a circle.'
From the *Taoist Canon*, quoted by Michael P. Garofolo.

Bugang is the Taoist ritualised walk or dance form, paced through a pattern reflecting a constellation, magic numbers square or other pattern, such as a circle. Based on the *Yubu* 'Steps of Yu' tradition, *Bugang* translates as 'Treading on the stars of the Dipper' or 'Pacing the guideline'. One of the most ancient forms of Taoist magic, it serves to dispel demons.

Yu was the legendary founder of the Xia Dynasty (c. 2070 – c. 1600 BCE). He controlled the Great Flood, but exerted himself so much he became lame, so emulating his limping gait was turned into the ritual walk. The *Luoshu* (Luo River) magic square is attributed to him. Also known as the *Jiugongtu*, Nine Halls Diagram, in this the Flood may represent Chaos, and Yu's walk through the Nine Halls an establishment of order. The lamed hero is of course a familiar mythic theme.

Incantations, visualisation of journeying through the heavens, and associated mudras were used throughout the *Bugang*. The idea of a Sacred Space is created and the practitioner may emulate the Supreme Unity, the deity Taiyi.

The walk along the Seven Stars of the Big Dipper is a practice of the *Shangqing* (Supreme Clarity) School. The stars of Ursa Major were drawn on a silk ribbon and, commanding the planets to encircle him, the Adept rose to the constellation, invoking the 'dark star' goddesses of the outer circle before proceeding to call upon the male residents of the Dipper, each star in turn.

The *Zhengyi Dao* (Way of Orthodox Unity) School uses the *Luoshu* square, with the Eight Trigrams around it. This was used liturgically for exorcism and purification, although it also had a place in sex magic rituals performed by couples.

Ge Hong's Baopuzi (c. 320 BCE) references the Paces of Yu, each pace equalling three steps, representing three levels of the Cosmos. *Yubu* is an element in the 'magic invisibility' system of *Qimen Dunjia*[5] (Irregular Gate, Hidden Stem); the gate is to the Otherworld and, approaching through use of the *Yubu*, the adept achieves invisibility to any malevolent entities or influences on the other side.

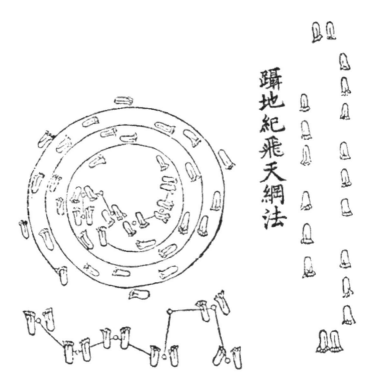

The Pace of Yu

Treading on Terrestrial Filaments, Soaring through Ursa Major

---

5 *Qimen Dunjia*, or *Qi Men Dun Jia*, can also translate as 'Mystical Door Escaping Technique' and was, so the story goes, used by Huang Ti to defeat Chi You. As a complex divination system it draws together astronomy, nine 'palaces' combined with the eight trigrams on a 3x3 square, the 5 Elements, Heaven, Human and Earth levels, Yin and Yang, the 10 Heavenly Stems and Eight Gods (Ba Shen) in a chart, with 1,080 configurations. It is grouped as one of the 'Three Rites' of Chinese divination, along with *Da Liu Ren* and *Tai Yin Shen Shu*, all three using divinatory boards.

The pattern of the constellation Ursa Major, the Great Bear, will be noticed in the diagram. Yu's famed ability to transform into a bear possibly simply means he walked the outline of the Great Bear.

The hexagram 63 is also formed with the steps, composed of the *Li* (Fire) and *Kan* (Water) trigrams. Hexagram 10 (Treading) may be formed as well.

HEXAGRAM 63

HEXAGRAM 10

After Completion, New Beginnings. Seeing through a veil. Crossing a river, keep moving.

Treading, Careful Stepping.

Marcel Granet has proposed that *Yubu* originated in the early shamanic tradition. This seems to be confirmed by recent archaeological discoveries of bamboo and silk manuscripts dating to c.217 BCE and c.168 BCE documenting *Yubu* practice (the *Rishi* and *Wushi'er Bingfang* texts).

Yubu continues to be performed in contemporary Taoist liturgical rituals, where the stepping methods are valued as an intrinsic foundation. From the shamanic roots of walking-forms as protective against demonic forces it was perhaps a natural progression to see that the art could be modified to work against aggressors in the physical world.

I am including here a section on the practice of Circle Walking from my book *Qi Gong: Learning the Way* (Green Magic, 2013) which can be referred to for further details on the physical techniques.

CIRCLE WALKING

'When you walk the circle for a time, the Hsien become present.'
A Tao-shih.

As the circle is a natural organic form to follow, humans have instinctively pursued circular forms in numerous activities. Sitting and dancing around a fire would have been one of the primal means to establish a sense of community, the Circle Dance being a communal tradition common to a variety of cultures, Celtic, Greek, Eastern European, North and South American Indian, Israeli and Islamic. It was sometimes known as a Sacred Circle Dance when performed for religious or meditative reasons. Mazes and spiral patterns were followed for ritual purposes by pre-Christian peoples. The Crane Dance was a means of solving the riddle of the Greek Labyrinth; the entrance to the underworld and emergence in ceremonial rebirth.

A circumambulation of parish boundaries by members of the community to mark the territory was known as Beating the Bounds, and is still extant in Cornwall. It could have been derived from the Roman Terminalia festival honouring the god of landmarks, Terminus.

There is also the magical practice of drawing a circle around oneself as a means of establishing a protection from obsession when entering altered states of consciousness. The Mandala (Sanskrit for magic circle) is a design used as a focal point in meditation, its circular structure symbolizing the path to individuation or as it could be phrased, Salvation. Its single central point is the goal of self realization and wholeness.

The true Taoist masters were the Tao-shih, dignitaries of the Tao. Through following the outline of a diagram in a form of a dance, the Taoist master could take possession of the symbol's forces. Very early shamanic practices included following dance patterns that would take the dancer into the sky, such as emulating the pattern of constellations, like the Big Dipper, Ursa Major. The practice of walking the circle is the common training method in Bagua Zhang, or eight trigram palm.

As a Taoist Qi cultivation method its aim is to seek union with the natural world, or 'The circumambulation of the Self' as Jung put it, in contrast to seated static meditation where the focus is inward. As the earth rotates around the sun and also around its own axis, so the practitioner is attuned to the greater cycles operating around us, 'a circle whose centre is everywhere and circumference nowhere'. (From *Liber XXIV Philosophorum*, by an anonymous author, dated anywhere from the 4th to 13th century. The quote has also been attributed to Nicholas of Cusa and Voltaire).

Dong Hai Chuan, the creator of the Bagua fighting method, was a member of the Quan Zhen (Complete Truth) Taoist sect, which can be traced back to the 8th Century Tang dynasty, part of the Dragon Gate or Long Men school. This sect practiced circle walking or Rotating in Worship of Heaven (Chuan T'ien Tsun).

Dong's genius was in adapting this meditative exercise to create an extremely effective fighting art. He was taught by two Taoist masters who apparently had him walk around a tree for 7 years, then around two trees in a figure eight for 2 years.

The encircling of a tree, post or pole is representative of circling the world's axis, or *axis mundi*, which symbolically connects heaven and earth. Dancing around a maypole is another example, or the use of the Totem pole. It is advised by some masters that if you walk around a tree as a circle walk exercise you should ask its permission; it's a living thing, after all.

The Taoists repeated mantras as they walked to focus the mind, creating stillness in motion. The pattern they followed was to walk three times very slowly around a circle, and then track an 'S' shape through the centre to continue in a reversed direction around the circle again. The circle therefore looked like the Tai Chi Yin/Yang diagram.

There are three circles used in Taoist magic representing the states of *Jing*, *Qi* and *Shen*: essence, energy and spirit. *Shen ling* = spiritual energy. Combining these circles results in a protective barrier for alchemy and ritual. The magic circle is actually envisaged as a sphere. Casting it begins with the adept facing East and ends in the same position. A clockwise circle attracts forces, counterclockwise banishes.

The 'Sword Hand' mudra is used to draw the circle if working in this manner and not following the 8 Animal Forms method of invocation. Entering or exiting the circle is then performed by cutting a doorway with the Sword Hand and sealing it with three horizontal passes, representing the *Ch'ien* trigram.

The Opposing Forces of the *Bagua* Circle, the arrangement of the eight fundamental trigrams of the I Ching, create a dynamic tension that resolves into harmony through the body of the practitioner. This is known as self-realization in other philosophies.

Your Own Personal Demon

Note that walking the double circle is a particularly powerful Dragon Gate formulation and is geared to putting one in touch with The Other. Again, this requires special measures of correct training and holding certain physical forms, rather than ambling around two circles haphazardly.

As I have mentioned, the Circle Walk was, and is, a means of dispelling demons. What it is correspondingly also reputed to do (and I say this guardedly, not to make any claims!) is to invoke a Personal Demon. The Personal Demon/Daimon might be posited to already be there waiting to manifest.

If there are Guardian Angels then in our dualistic world we could expect Guardian Demons.

The cartoons of an angel on one shoulder, a devil on the other, may have a hint of truth.

The Diabolic Intelligences of the *I Ching*

'The best way to live in the multiverse is to think carefully about
how you live your life in this one.'
Rowan Hooper.

THE *I Ching* in its form of a magic system rather than a philosophical
or literary work enfolds numerology with spirit contact and
interdimensional exploration as well as divination and sigilisation.
There are other ancient Chinese divinatory systems, the *Ling Qi Jing*
for one, dating to 200 to 400 CE and written by an unknown author,
which consists of 125 oracular poems and commentaries that uses a
set of 12 'spirit tokens' for consultation. The earliest form of Chinese
writing is found in the Oracle Bone Script, characters on animal
bones or turtle plastrons in pyromantic divination. Of these, the *I
Ching* is by far the most well-known.

The philosophical side of the *I Ching* may have predated the
divinatory, as Thomas Cleary believes, in which case it is applied as
a system for expanding awareness of internal states and increasing
adaptability. A humanistic interpretation of spirits as inner complexes
isn't far removed from the Taoist conception of deities residing in the
body.

An imperative element in the *I Ching* is time. Stephen Karcher
has put forward the intriguing idea that in the ancient world, time
units were demonic images, and movement through time entailed
confrontation with the demons of the unknown. This was a concern
of the *I Ching*, whose key term *I* or *Yi* can be interpreted as 'disruptive'.
In *Which Way I Fly is Hell: Divination and the Shadow of the West*, Karcher
insists that the *I Ching* in itself is not a demon but rather a maker of
demons, meaning that we can experience demonic force as informative
and regulating, and can establish a field of communication between
ourselves and it, finding our way back to a realisation of our essential
spirit selves. Everett Kleinjans has also used the word 'diabolic' in
association with the *I Ching* in his paper 'I Ching – Book of Symbolic
Communication' (1987). By distinguishing the word 'diabolic' in its

original Greek meaning as 'thrown apart, divided, separated', with 'symbolic' signifying 'unification', an aspect of the *I Ching* is the manifesting of symbolic and diabolic communication. These powers form, as it were, the living soul of the book. The powers have also been taken to be ancestral spirits. Ancestors can be interpreted as familial, but we could decipher them as relating to the reader's previous personas, past selves rather than familial spirits, which would quite likely include demonic parts or potentials to be 'exorcised'. We can embrace the errors of the past and synthesise our demons if we recognise them for what they are.

The philosophy of Taoism is an integral part of the *I Ching*, with its concepts of Yin and Yang, the harmony of opposites, and its observation of continual change. Yin and Yang can be compared to the binary notation of 0 and 1. In fact Liebniz, inventor of the binary code, studied the *I Ching*. The binary polarity of Yes/No answers to questions were indicated by an unbroken/broken line, which evolved with an increase in the complexity of the world and correspondingly with questions. Events in the *I Ching* are reflected spatially in Heaven and Earth but also in Time.

The demonic side of the oracle is in what it shares with computers, its predictive capacity, because human life is unpredictable, and human thought and creativity respond to this unpredictability.

According to contemporary physics we are part of a superimposed quantum multiverse of many interacting worlds. At least, that is one theory. In a many-worlds interpretation, every decision has consequences beyond what is directly considered or experienced. Any decision involving probability causes the universe to branch. This is an enticing concept to consider when using a divinatory method such as the *I Ching* or *Book of Changes*. (S.Y. Wong has commented that it should be 'The Book of Change' rather than 'Changes', as change is the only reality).

The three levels of lines in a trigram can be related to the Three Powers or *San Cai*; Heaven, Human and Earth. Accordingly, we are placed between Heaven and Earth. Two trigrams in combination provide a hexagram. Jay G. Williams has said that the hexagrams are not unlike Platonic forms, as being basic formulae for events. Plato's world of change, however, is one of shadows and illusions, the true world being changeless. The *I Ching* incorporates movement into the nature of reality, as hexagrams are in a continual state of flux. (Williams also makes a cogent point that we should not split philosophy into Western and Eastern, recognising instead only wisdom). The eight *I Ching* trigrams multiplied present the 64 hexagrams.

Traditionally the hexagrams were composed by a throw of 50 yarrow stalks, or 3 coins. Jung in his 1949 foreword to the Wilhelm translation wrote that '... according to the old tradition, it is "spiritual agencies", acting in a mysterious way, that make the yarrow stalks give a meaningful answer.' The Chinese coins have square holes in them, representing earth surrounded by the circle of heaven. The coins are thrown six times to produce the lines. The hexagrams were adopted by followers of internal alchemy to symbolise the processes of that art, and some *Tai Chi* teachers associate them with movements throughout the Form.

The eight by eight grid of the *I Ching* interpretive table could be compared to a chess board with its 64 black and white (Yin and Yang) squares. The Chinese character *Ko* means 'a check pattern formed from crossed lines' and is phonetically identical to another character that means 'to change, transform'.

In a hexagram, the lower trigram is the inner aspect, the upper trigram is the outer aspect, relating the inner personal condition to the outer external situation. Much in the way that Western practitioners of sympathetic magic constructed tables of correspondences, the eight trigrams are associated with a variety of qualities and archetypes.

The trigrams can be considered as paired; *Ch'ien* and *K'un* are the most important, symbolising the primal energy that gave birth to everything, Yang and Yin respectively. *K'an* and *Li*, Water and Fire, are also important as alchemical symbols. *Ken* and *Chen* equal Stillness and Movement; *Sun* and *Tui*, Infiltration and Dissipation.

Through divination it could be said we engage in an interaction with the non-linear language of the psyche. Divinatory methods provide a means of bridging the linear mode of thought to access holistic patterning. Such techniques momentarily occupy or distract the rational critical mind, allowing access to deep levels of consciousness – an intuitive perception of order out of chaos.

Marie-Louise von Franz, a student of Jung, was possibly the first person to make a connection between the 64 hexagrams and the 64 codons of DNA, since which there have been books on the subject by

Schonberger, Yan and Walter. It adds another intriguing level to the concept of the *I Ching* as a living entity.

Finally, the representation of the 64 hexagrams as a magic square, sometimes pictured with a surrounding circle, has a talismanic aspect which, if hardly considered popularly, nevertheless has been and is used in conjuration practices. What is being conjured into manifestation depends on the individual's intent.

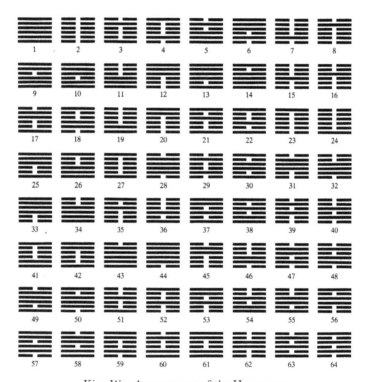

King Wen Arrangement of the Hexagrams

The Demon Land

'The earth is breathing, full of rest and sleep.' (From Mahler's *Das Lied von der Erde*, a setting of Chinese poems.)

Searching the Mountains for Demons by Zheng Zhong
(active c. 1612 – 1648).

THE GOD Erlang depicted here defeated demons and a flood-causing dragon on Mount Guankou in Sichuan. He was a representation of Li Bing, a governor of Chengdu in the 3ʳᵈ Century BCE who created an irrigation system and helped control flooding, combined with a hunting deity who could control mountain creatures.

China has a long history of being one of the countries most prone to the whole range of natural disasters, including floods, earthquakes and typhoons. The ancient attitude of linking such incidents to a divine judgment on human conduct was rejected during the Maoist years, when nature became an adversary, something to be controlled and defeated. 'Earthquakes cannot frighten us, the people will certainly conquer nature' ran one slogan.

Demons were not necessarily held accountable for tragic natural events, although there were specific tales of demonic entities involved in some cases. Shuimu Niangniang is a water demon or demon goddess who was responsible for submerging Sizhou (in Anhui Province today), an ancient city, under Hongze Lake in 1574 CE. There's one colourful story of her fighting Wang Lingquan, the Taoist Supreme God, and his army of celestial warriors, at the behest of the Water Elephant. The land is the battlefield, rather than some heavenly realm. She goes into combat alongside Tuhuogi, a fire demon, 5000 sailors, magic tortoises and Eastern sea crabs, attacking with torrents of fire and water. Shuimu creates tidal waves from the five great lakes, flooding the plains, but is eventually overpowered. She is presently sealed under a mountain in Xuyi District.

Another story is of Yu the Great, who halted a flood by defeating the river demon Wuzhiqi who had caused it and appeared in the form of a monkey.

The Demon Land is a term that appears in various forms and is applied to areas within the country occupied by opposing forces such as the Tartars, to a province where the occupants were involved in communicating with entities (see Spence, p. 101: Mrs. Montague Beaucham '...had lived in one of the particular provinces known as demon land'), to a foreign land, especially in the experience of Chinese migrants to America, and to a supernatural realm, as with the popular story of Bai Suzhen, a white snake from the Land of Demons who transforms herself into a woman and does good deeds in the human world, even meeting Kuan Yin amiably. A theme of the tale is that not all demons are evil.

Daemon (sic) Land, *Shouhu tudi*, is translated back into English as Guard the Land.

The Wall is China's most recognisable topographical feature. A series of fortifications begun as early as the 7th century BCE, the major part of the Great Wall dates to the Ming Dynasty. It was designed for border control, defense and transportation, as well as signalling from the watch towers.

The setting up of walls is a current fixation of the new nationalist wave, where The Wall separates and delineates a nation, as national identity. It proposes that those within the wall are protected from an enemy without and promotes the idea of needing to be isolated and insulated from a contaminating Other. Walls defined as such diminish the status of the excluded from human individuals to a collective alienated and demonised horde. The idea in vogue during the early 20th century among occultists, and promoted as part of the current of right-wing identification which we are on the brink of unfortunately repeating if not careful, was to separate traditions and study only native ones. In a global interrelated world, traditions now choose us. The shadow of patriotism is one of the worst demons.

The Great Wall
Photo by Arnold Wright, 1908.

A wall can obviously be either an actual physical structure or a conceptual boundary, but it need not be negatively exclusionary. It might also be the aesthetic of enclosed spaces, of mysteries guarded; garden walls and dry-stone walls may enhance and romance a vista.

We exist in *Yang Jian*, the living world of reality, between Heaven and Hell. *Yin Jian*, the underworld of spirits, occupies some precarious other dimension. Our human realm is composed of time, space and matter. At the dawn of time, nature was in opposition to us, and full of demons that had to be tamed in order for us to survive. Now we live in comfort but are in opposition to nature as we pollute it. The new demons find their source in ourselves.

Taoist ideals in regard to the environment can be found to be expressed explicitly through the medium of current Western ecological theory. Adverse effects upon the land are countered by or diverted through the use of such arts as *Feng Shui*. The land is a part of the body, we are immersed in it, and spiritual influences are both in and around the earth. Our landscape is both the backdrop or stage for our performance on it, and a component in our identity, but not as the draining absorption of nationalism would have it.

There is an ambivalence to nature. In one way, it is benevolent, humanised and domesticated. But on the other hand, it represents a demonic wilderness, untameable and uninhabitable. Demons were/ are found in 'wild, deserted, uncivilized (...) spaces marked by death or the idea of wandering' (de Rolley). The malevolence of nature demons had to be counteracted with ritual techniques, which was a parallel to the early material process of cultivating the land.

The Christian notion of exorcism has similarities to Chinese/ Eastern shamanic practice, with spirits ordered into categories, capable of inhabiting the land as well as individuals, and the method of driving them out including prayer/incantations and circular walks around the area they possess. Christian Evangelism began using the terms Spiritual Warfare, Strategic Level Spiritual Warfare, Spiritual Mapping and Territorial Spirits in the early 1990s with the rise of the New Apostolic Movement.

It can be said that cities are a part of nature, in the same way that nests, burrows and other habitats are for non-human creatures. Evil spirits ruling a town, community, city or even a country are known as Territorial Spirits or Strategic Level demons. There are two other levels; Ground Level demons possess people, and Occult Level demons give power to witches and sorcerers. Seeking the location and names of the demons is Spiritual Mapping. This whole model of an ordered approach to dealing with chaotic entities is, it has been speculated, possibly derived from the Eastern Shamanic model, from Christian missionary interaction with common folk magic traditions (see Ooi, 2006).

Deities protecting cities (*Ch'eng-huang*) also acted as guides to the dead. To help a soul out of Hell, a Taoist priest had to inform the city deity of this intention of soul retrieval by providing a document. The title King or Duke was given to these deities by the end of the 10th century CE, and they were celebrated with feast days. T'u-ti, a subordinated deity to a city god, would be in charge of a specific area, a street or building.

Exorcism is not just of spirits; it can also be thought of as adjusting large scale energy patterns. There is according to the Taoist view an environmental energy based in the earth, accumulating underground that can be injurious to humans and other living things, although it has its reason for being (volcanoes release pressure). This environmental energy can affect the human body to the extent that a form of exorcism is needed for the individual to be 'cleared' of it. It can be compared to the Schumann Resonances, also known as The Schumann Resonance, electromagnetic waves generated by lightning discharges and thought of in New Age circles as the planet's 'energy pulse'. There have been attempts to connect this to a corresponding human energetic resonance, discredited by the scientific community.

The landscape being engendered as feminine, deriving from the Gaia hypothesis (which Lovelock himself disavowed) has identified 'the masculine' Yang with the consensual world of the material and equated 'the feminine' Yin with an ethical value, environmentalism (with the Earth itself being regarded as female), mysticism and non-aggression, even non-competitiveness. This is undoubtedly a very selective reading; we can just as easily see hills, mountains and volcanoes as Yang-representative features. Nonetheless, the sentiment is there – a viable concern in reclaiming a sensibility for nature.

Geomancy or the study of earth is a focus on having a sense of place and living in harmony with one's surroundings. The geomantic art of Feng Shui translates as Wind and Water, that is symbolically, the flow of energy through natural and constructed landscape. (The term 'Astro-geomancy' includes astronomy in the subject matter, and on occasion astrology, although the latter is treated with caution, if not even scepticism, by the Taoist. 'My fate is within me, not in the heavens' is a Taoist alchemist saying). *Feng shui* is an eminently practicable art and should never have been interpreted solely as a simplified fashion statement.

Environmental energy may not be entirely a natural form; earthworks, building sites, electromagnetic transmission from pylons and power stations are detrimental too. There is as well an energy from the sky or space, such as weather changes that affects us.

Certain locations are credited as being 'power spots' (*qi-di*), with 'dragon veins' (*lung-mai*) running through them, such as with China's Five Sacred Mountains (named in the next section, on Talismanic

Magic). Sacred caves were considered labyrinths (Kaltenmark) with a great treasure such as a text or teaching at the centre.

One example of using the magical power of a specific place is the practice of *Zung saang gei* which requires placing a hair in a selected location in order to extend someone's life. Tina Leung, the Hong Kong actress, was reported as having performed this in 1998. The maximum number of years she could hope for was 12. She died exactly 12 years later.

Within buildings and other structures, the Chinese view is much in accordance with the idea that enclosed spaces serve to store impressions psychically, hence ghosts, and that when some strong feelings linger, the astral or emotional body gets attached to places. Room temperature falling inexplicably is a classic indicator of an other-worldly presence. Talismans are used in *feng shui* to divert *Sha* (evil Qi) and ghosts. The magician's red rope can be employed to protect spaces, being joined in a circle, or constructed as the Ruji, a Sacred Knot. Stone tablets are used to gather positive energy and ward off evil, placed at main doors, three-way junctions, river banks and ponds. The cardinal points are acknowledged in clearing spaces: the north-easterly direction is as previously mentioned the 'demon gate' where demons pass through.

It was once believed that in order to ensure a bridge was stable the names of living people should be written down, stuck to a wooden pile and sunk into the river, imbuing the bridge with the named spirits. This was called 'stealing souls' (see Kuhn). A more sinister and recent (2007) rumour had it that children were going to be buried under a viaduct for the same reason (Zhiyuan), although it was dismissed as preposterous.

An early interpretation of there being a spiritual element in landscape was present in Eastern Asian art, with Taoism an influence. In the West this attribution flowered with the Romantic tradition. Landscape as a term was initially used in English as a reference to works of art, first dated to 1598. (Depictions of actual views are more accurately called topological views.)

From the 16th century European artists focused on landscape in paintings with human figures becoming secondary features. This again is an attribution in Chinese and specifically Taoist influenced artworks. Claude Lorraine (1600 to 1682) modified landscapes into a vision of the sublime, influencing English landscape gardeners and giving rise to the ideal of the 'picturesque', i.e. like a picture of Claude's.

In *Environmental Aesthetics*, Berleant writes of participatory engagement in which the environment (which comes from the Old French word meaning 'to encircle') is engaging and continuous with the observer, rather than the more traditional view of a 'disinterested attention' in aesthetic response. Participation mystique, or mystical participation, on the other hand, the term Jung derived from Levy-Bruhl, is related to projection, a psychological connection binding subject to object. In this way we 'make sense' of our involvement with the environment. The protective spirit or *genius loci* of a place is usually referred to now as a distinct atmosphere rather than indicating a guardian, although Chinese folk-belief claims trees have the ability to become protecting spirits when tied with red cloth strips, and are identified with the social body. If a branch is cut someone in the area near will die.

With the Earth idealised as Garden of Eden, an originally pristine paradise, the reason for its Fall has through Biblical interpretation been laid upon Women/The Serpent. In contrast, the Creator Goddess of the Chinese Earth is a quasi-demonic (if only in appearance) Snake Goddess.

Nuwa: Earth and Snake Goddess
from *Myths and Legends of China* by E.T.C. Werner, 1922.

The Garden, that icon fixated upon as symbolic of a purer world, is wrestled from Nature's grasp by continual effort. Most of the classic Chinese gardens were unfortunately destroyed along with the Taoist temples during the Cultural Revolution.

The serpent hybrid is often depicted as female (although in this image the gender is less explicit), a figuration symptomatic of the demonising of women peculiarly found in most cultures: women either in shadow or as Shadow.

The Temptation of Eve
John Roddam Spencer Stanhope, 19th c.

A whisper in the right ear, while Eve's left hand holds, it would appear, two fruit; apart from any obvious sexual connotations, there is a devious little message hidden here. The suggestions of one's demon do not have to be followed but may lead down an ultimately enlightening path.

Cathay, China itself as 'the ultimate Other' (to quote Zhang Longxi), has not only been a land that has fought ceaseless external battles to maintain its boundaries and identity, but one of internal tensions.

'Who governs his body governs the country', (*The Taoist Body*). The Emperor had to be in harmony with his land. He dwelt in the Hall of Light or House of the Calendar, a building designed to represent the universe, where according to cyclic, directional and seasonal correspondences he moved from room to room, being thereby united with his realm. The responsibility for ensuring the welfare of the country lay in his personal health and conduct. This conjunction of the Ruler with the Land finds an echo in the Arthurian mythology of the Waste Land. Physical embodiment, a full connection with the land rather than dreamy transcendence, is a relationship with nature ideally pursued and embraced by the Taoist.

The China of the magicians, an imaginary China, is in opposition to the real-world industrialised landscape where the air in some urban environs is so heavily polluted that wearing a surgical mask becomes necessary and windows cannot be opened. Here we have a demonic landscape in physical manifestation.

Another contrary aspect of the Chinese world to the average Westerner is the inversion of the points of the compass, where North becomes South and East becomes West (see illustration in the Taoist Alchemy, p. 119).

While interiorised idealism was projected outwardly to create the Chinese garden, or in painting to reflect the working of Tao, *Neijing Tu* is an Inner Landscape diagram (see page 103) illustrating principles of Internal Alchemy and that 'The human body is an image of a country'. All received copies are from the Beijing White Cloud Temple and date to 1886. The original provenance is unknown.

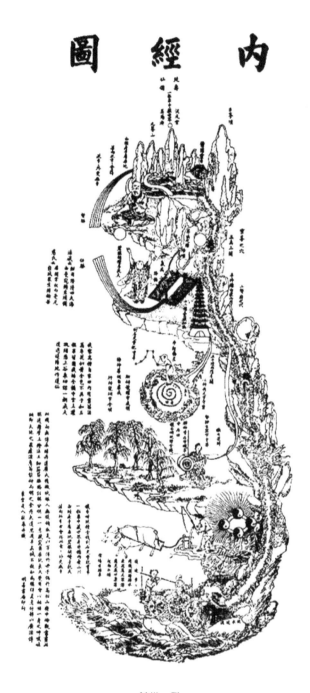

Neijing Tu

Demonifuge Talismanic Magic

Cheng-i tao, the Way of Right Unity, is a term for all Taoist schools using talismans and amulets in their practice. Another term is *Fu-lu p'ai*, School of Talismans. *Fu-lu* were originally contracts written on pieces of metal or paper and split in two, one for each party involved. The idea of a contract was upheld in the use of *fu-lu* in negotiating contact with deities. Fu talismans are, to be correct, only employed by Taoist adepts with years of training behind them. Protection from demons and warding off illness are also their main employment. The magic square of three, the *Luo Shu* or Luo River writing mentioned in pre-Han and Han documents, was a secret talisman preceding the *Bagua* and hexagrams and fundamental to their meaning.

Fu-lu were traditionally considered to be an energetic or condensed form of clouds. A style of talismanic script is called *Yun-chuan*, 'Cloud Writing', due to its curved lines resembling the outline of cirrus clouds. As object, or symbol drawn or written, talismans have a dual existence on Earth and in Heaven.

Preparation is required to properly construct them: fasting to purify one's internal body, and a ritual bath to cleanse the external. Incense is lit and the intention must be focused to the exclusion of all other thoughts. An incantation is employed and the talisman is blessed and sealed.

The pens and inks used for writing talismans are specifically selected, with red ink on yellow paper being most commonly employed. A circle may be inscribed around the design, then dotted in the centre to focus the intent.

A typical ritual for using a talisman would consist after due preparation of using the power of the four elements. Incantations would be used to charge a receptacle filled with water (Air and Water combined). The magical talisman would be constructed, charged with an incantation and burnt (Fire element). The ashes (Earth) are placed in the water and used for healing or blessing. *Fu* are sealed and authorized with a stamp. This can even be a visualized stamp.

As an example of candle magic, unused, preferably beeswax candles are 'dressed' or charged with the intent. Oil for this purpose is rubbed from the top of the candle to midway, then from the bottom up to the middle. The objective is written on yellow paper, folded three times, then lit and placed on the altar dish. Alternatively, instead of being burnt the paper can be placed under the candle, which is allowed to burn down completely.

Alchemical Qi Gong (Energy Work) is also used during the construction of talismans, with the lower, middle and upper *Tan Tien* or Energy Gates being sequentially activated (navel, heart and Third Eye point between the brows to give a rough description of location). An entity can be summoned to energize the talisman, or it can be traced in the air with the tip of a magical sword, an incense stick, the hand or other instrument. It can be enclosed in a ball of energy and sent to its destination. The method employed by some other traditions of locking a spirit into an object such as a talisman is advised against in Taoist magic.

Christine Mollier notes 'four Taoist talismans to expel the *gu* poison' and 'ten demonifuge talismans', amongst many others, in *Buddhism and Taoism Face to Face*. The exorcistic talismans of the Three Sources of Radiance from the *Shang-ch'ing t'ien-p'eng fu-mo ta-fa* (Great Rites of the T'ien-p'eng Spirit of Shang-ch'ang for Subduing Demons) can be found in Boltz's *A Survey of Taoist Literature* (p. 36) and *Ch'ing-wei* tradition talismans are illustrated on page 40.

Boltz writes that talismans as 'embodiments of divine power were largely sought for demonifuge purposes' in the Sung Dynasty, as well as incantations.

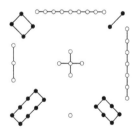

4	9	2
3	5	7
8	1	6

Luo Shu Talisman   Magic Number Square

TALISMANIC HAND FORM

The Yin-Yang double hand seal can be used as a method for meditatively charging talismans. Three fingers of the left hand are placed over the four fingers of the right hand, palms down, with the little finger of the left hand under the right hand fingers. The left thumb is placed between the right thumb and palm. It is used to open or imprint and close or seal a talisman.

THE DIAGRAM OF THE TRUE FORM OF THE FIVE MOUNTAINS

The mountains were symbolic of routes to seclusion, an escape from the distraction of the mundane world below them, but these routes were fraught with danger. At certain times they could be 'open' or 'closed'. Talismans for journeys helped to orientate the traveller, like a compass, providing a sacred order.

The *Wuyue Zhenxing Tu* was a talisman carried by Taoists going into the mountains, providing protection from demons taking human form and misleading travellers, and guarding against wild animals too. The Taoist also carried a nine-inch mirror on his back that could show a demon's true form reflected in it, nine being a solar number. Mirrors show the true form of all things.

The *Wuyue Zhenxing Tu* was originally received by Ge Hong from his master, Zheng Yin. Ge Hong lived near present day Nanjing during the Eastern Jin dynasty (CE 317-420). He was known as Baopuzi, the Master who Embraces Simplicity. The legend is that for the final stage of his cultivation of immortality he was in a cave for 49 days, and when he ascended his clothes turned into thousands of butterflies. The cave became known as the Butterfly Cave.

When the Five Mountain Diagram is placed in a home, it should be located on an altar.

THE EAST MOUNTAIN: Tai Shan, located in San Dong Tai An. Takes care of wealth and fortune, birth and death. (Top right corner of diagram as viewed)

THE SOUTH MOUNTAIN: Heng Shan, in Heng Nan province. Cares for the sun, moon and stars, as well as aquatic creatures. (Bottom right)

THE MIDDLE MOUNTAIN: Song Shan in He Nan province. Looks after hills and mountains, and domestic animals. (Middle)

THE WEST MOUNTAIN: Hua Shan in Shaanxi. Protects gold, silver and bronze, plus flying creatures. (Bottom left)

THE NORTH MOUNTAIN: Heng Shan in Shanxi. Rivers, seas and four-legged wild animals are under this mountain's protection. (Top left)

From the *Pao P'u-tzu*:

'The mountain power in the form of a little boy hopping backward on one foot likes to harm people. If you hear a human voice at night in the mountains loudly talking, its name is Ch'i. By knowing this name and shouting it out, you will prevent it harming you ...

'There is another mountain power, in the shape of a drum, coloured red and also with just one foot. This one is named Hui. Yet another power has the form of a human being nine feet tall...

'Whenever one of these appears, shout its name. It will not then dare to harm you.'

The Diagram of the True Form of the Five Mountains
(Wuyue Zhenxing Tu)

Observations of Taoist Psychospiritual Theory

'What men call the shadow of the body is not the shadow of the body, but is the body of the soul.' Oscar Wilde, *A House of Pomegranates*.

THIS IS not a grimoire, in the sense of a manual for invoking demons (though maybe the term 'Book of Shadows' would not be inaccurate), and Taoist techniques inclusive of its forms of alchemy do not engage in such invocations as a rule. Contact with paranormal phenomena arising spontaneously, in whatever manner or form dependent upon the individual, is reputed to be a *process* of the methods I describe in the following sections. As ever, balance is the safeguard.

For those drawn to alchemical/ritual working, the Shadow emerging at some point is as natural an outcome as for those who are not engaged in such practices; with the former, there is more preparation in being able to deal with it. To phrase it in another manner: demons may be thought of as constellations of what we contend with.

With the two magical modes of ritual and alchemy, ritual is broadly outward based, a performance that engages the participant, and may involve others, in forms to impress and change the surrounding atmosphere. It clears a space in anticipation of some Other entering (or leaving). Alchemy is inward, where even the external style is characteristically a more introverted and self-seeking endeavour. Ritual clears, alchemy sublimates. (There again, we may also make a categorisation of 'alchemical ritual', as with Circle Walking for instance.) The alchemical exercises outlined or suggested here are heuristic techniques which are included as examples of the kind of methodology undertaken by adepts.

The paradigm of a substitute or alternative spiritualised body is found in a variety of traditions. This vessel is either ready-formed or capable of being created/developed; in Taoism and Vajrayana we find 'the diamond body' as one term for it, and there is as well the 'alchemical embryo', a form that holds the adept's intention for spiritual growth. Whether known as the Etheric body, Psychic body, Subtle body or the Body of Light, from esoteric Hinduism to Gurdjieff and Ouspensky's *Fourth Way*, a psychospiritual physiology finds expression as a medium for the individual relating to higher planes. The implication is you can't get there in an earth body.

Like an electronic Other or VR 'avatar', the Subtle Body may overlay the physical and consist of virtual organs and energetic channels as Occult Anatomy. This etheric physiology conveys and stores breath, or Qi, as a consequence of visualisation and active exercise such as Qi Gong; in the latter case the Subtle Body may be activated indirectly. The theory behind acupuncture which is held to have a demonstrable effect through manipulating energetic channels may be debated for being unscientific according to 'method', but there is a wealth of documentation attesting to its efficacy.

Part of the unease in the scientific community is the representation of an *internal energy*, whether called Qi or Ki or Kundalini. If we substitute the *feeling* of wellbeing, vitality and aliveness for those terms then we simply bypass that controversy. Feelings are not conducive to scientific method, but most of us have them.

Taoist energetic exercises are 'circular', and the energetic circulatory system has been copiously annotated to the clarity of a medical text. This is understandable as the purely physical was not separated from the subtle in Taoist medicine. The Kundalini Psychosis mentioned earlier – yogic energetic practice resulting in mental disorders – is not an experience found in any equivalent form in the Taoist texts because energy is not visualized as proceeding in one direction only (up through the body and into the head in the yogic case) but as circulated and balanced.

The effect of demons or deities internally is, or should be, dealt with on this counterpart level and therefore defused from becoming a physical problem. That is the beauty and elegance of the Taoist system.

A representation of universal order and indicative of humanity's place in it, 'Macrocosmic Man' (as it has been popularly labelled) was an illustration of the human form transposed onto and into a plan of the universe; Da Vinci's *Vitruvian Man* occupies a similar position, making a statement about our relationship to geometry, and the power of numbers. Yudelove entertains this comparativism further in *The Tao and the Tree of Life* (p.109) by corresponding Taoist theories with the Qabalah. So, the 32 paths of the Qabalistic Tree of Life could be matched to the 32 prime meridians in the Chinese model of occult anatomy.

Sun Si-Miao's 32 exorcistic drugs may also be associated (see Taoist Alchemy chapter); a coincidence of numbers can at least lead to some interesting comparisons between traditions if we do not mind engaging with the speculative. For example, someone was bound to notice that 32 is the 'mirror' of 23, and then we enter Robert Anton Wilson territory. Numerical synchronicities are a world of brain spin, so I'll leave it there.

There are opposing forces in mind and body that can be classified as Inward and Outward and Upward and Downward tensions: the pull and push of contrasting directions. These are:

1. Wisdom opposed to Knowledge.

Acquiring learning and inner reflection: The processes of being informed. 'To attain knowledge, add things every day. To attain wisdom, remove things every day.' (Lao Tzu).

In our acquisitive culture, wisdom is seen as Knowing Things; to know more and more. Cleverness is not always equal to Wisdom, though, just as Intelligence does not of necessity equate to Compassion. There is a point to gaining information, but also to sifting through it critically and simplifying the mass of what we are confronted with.

2. Gravity opposed to Enlightenment.

Enlightenment here means as applied to 'Lightening the Body'. The *p'o* soul opposes the *hun* in a downward direction; gravity is a 'grave' force and pulls us to the earth especially as we get older.

Mentally as well as physically we can find our bodies getting heavier (not in the sense of physical weight gain), slower, harder to move. The *hun* soul meanwhile strives to reach upward just as the Taoist path to immortality aims to lighten the physical being through alchemical methods, inclusive of the more recondite aspects of Tai Chi. We may not achieve the state of immortality, or even wish to follow that route, but some of its methods are useful.

There is too the paradoxical idea of the body within the mind. This seemingly illogical concept is a reversal of the usual experience that we are contained physically, our consciousness enclosed within the strictures of form. One Taoist position which is generally found in other culturally diverse teachings of mysticism is to turn the viewpoint around: to see the body as if surrounded by mind. Travelling 'through the looking glass' is known here as Crossing the Dragon Gate.

As with some other practices, this is not recommended for those likely to be adversely affected by a questioning of relative reality. The danger is in whether the experience is a projected illusion or sedentary wishing, or as far as can be ascertained an objective issue. Not that it has previously been acceptable to scientism, but stranger things are now in the process of becoming established.

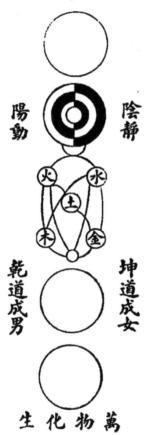

The idea is to imagine this image in three dimensions rather than two, so it is substantially spherical and holographic.

From the original hermaphroditism or integrated bisexual nature of the Divine there was a split, a separation of male and female. In Chinese symbolism the *Tai Chi T'u* is a depiction of the principle of Yin and Yang, but the meaning is more subtle than a sharp delineation or division into opposites; as a harmoniously interacting blend, one form turning into the other endlessly, complementing each other.

The Primal Spirit that moved across the Cosmos pervaded everything with its essence. The gods were androgynous, and so were their creations.

Ch'en T'uan's Diagram of the Supreme Ultimate, 10th century CE.

Taoist Alchemy

'Everything arises in this way, opposites from their opposites.'
Plato, *Phaedo*.

SCHIPPER MAKES an unusual statement in *The Taoist Body*: 'The concentration of one's vital forces, maintained through self-perfection, makes one a formidable demon before one becomes a gentle and beneficial power' (page 43). He doesn't elaborate on what he means by this, so it is open to conjecture until one faces the experience of synthesising one's own dark double.

Alchemy (*Lian jin shu*) as the transmutation of dark energy or matter into light can be applied to resolving inner demons, whether framed as psychological constructs or independent entities, and externally in changing one's life space. That phase of the Great Work called the *nigredo* or 'dark night of the soul' is the confrontation with the shadow which leads to the *coniunctio*, the union of opposites.

The Taoist Canon is the main source for alchemical works, although not all Chinese alchemy is Taoist.

Obed Simon Johnson's *A Study of Chinese Alchemy* (1928) was one of the first accounts in English. The practice consists of two branches, *Waidan* (external, with minerals and metals being used to make an elixir) and *Neidan* (internal, where through meditative exercises the process of transformation occurs within the alchemist's own body). The pursuit of immortality is a major aim, although Chuang-tzu is critical of the pursuit of longevity. To him, life and death are a natural process of change. Our energy doesn't disappear upon death but returns to its source.

Also, the Taoist alchemical texts sometimes seemingly contradict themselves; the *Cantong qi* at one point warns against meditative and breathing practices as not being the way to true realisation.

Points of translation may be an issue, and the Commentaries that have been appended to the texts over the centuries do not necessarily make them clearer.

WAIDAN

The elixirs of the Waidan alchemists consisted of a few poisonous materials such as mercury and lead. Committing ritual suicide as a conscious release of their spirit-bodies in order to become an immortal is a counter-argument to the common perception that the alchemists killed themselves by accident, and has been put forward by Strickmann (1979). They would have been competent in knowing the nature of what they were dealing with. By the time of the Six Dynasties (during the age of the Three Kingdoms, Jin, and Southern and Northern Dynasties, i.e. 220-589 CE), there were certainly records being kept of the toxicity of some plants and minerals.

Self-mummification may have been another form of immortality pursued, such as practiced by Buddhist monks (*Sokushinbutsu*), an extreme course of asceticism including eating tree bark and resin.

Magic mushrooms (*ling chih*), which meant magic in a literal sense, including fly agaric (Amanita muscaria) and *xiaojun* ('laughing mushroom', perhaps Gymnopilus junonius or Panaeolus papilionaceus) were most possibly used by Taoist alchemists searching for the elixir of immortality, and Joseph Needham for one has proposed that mushrooms *were* the elixir (1974). Fungi are generally characterised as Yin essence. The adept's cap is a fungoid form, decorated with Yang symbols. Cone-shaped mushrooms, however, are regarded as phallic, and therefore Yang. Incidentally, Terence McKenna thought that the 'Forbidden Fruit', rather than being an apple, was the Psilocybe cubensis mushroom.

Five Minerals (*wushisan*) or Cold Food powder (*hanshisan*) was used medicinally and as a stimulant. The Seven Sages of the Bamboo Grove, my favourite group of dissolute Taoists, used it, and it is detailed in the *Baopuzi*. One list of the ingredients is realgar, cinnabar, orpiment, alum and laminar malachite, but there are various others. It was popular from the time of the Six Dynasties to the Tang. The name 'Cold Food' comes from the means of counteracting its pyretic effect, by eating cold food and bathing in cold water.

During the Tang Dynasty the acupuncturist and herbalist Sun Si-Miao wrote the 30 volume *Prescriptions Worth a Thousand Gold Ducats*. Volume 2 contained a list of 32 drugs prescribed against demons, along with 13 acupuncture 'Ghost Points' to treat possession. It is tempting to speculate on a combined treatment of herbalism with acupuncture given the number 32, which is the sum of the major meridians: 12 paired organ channels and 8 'psychic' vessels.

SPIRITS OF SPIRITS

The aforementioned Seven Sages of the Bamboo Grove, *Chu-lin ch'i-hsien* or *Zhulinqixian*, were a group of scholars, musicians, artists and poets who embraced a return to nature as both an idealistic escape from the repression of government and personally in the form of spontaneity and freedom of expression. Several were linked to the *Qingtan* (Pure Conversation) movement of Taoism.

The use of alcohol exemplified their hedonistic lifestyle but was also indicative of holding a different perspective, or consciousness — drunkenness as shamanic ecstasy, trance-forms/transforming, entering other dimensions. Ecstatic intoxication, the drunkenness of the Spirit, is found in various threads of mysticism, Sufism being one, and while it is most often taken rhetorically, using alcohol as a physical means of accessing a differing state also has its place.

NEIDAN

The 'demonic' aspect of alchemy is that it dares to challenge what is accepted in nature. Mortality is supplanted by immortality. The fixed status of elements is overturned. Nature's rule book is questioned and ultimately revoked. This contesting of authority has historically been a lonely determination of women and men with singular minds.

Isabelle Robinet's *The World Upside Down* is particularly a work of initiation, where the principle of *diandao*, reversal or inversion, is presented with wonderful clarity. Transgression is an alchemical rhetorical device: 'The alchemical language is a mirror play.' 'Reverse' breathing, the reversal of the Great Circulation of *qi*, and the 'destructive' (a misleading interpretation) cycle in the Five Processes, are a few of the methods employed.

Both physical immortality and the transmutation of base materials into precious ones are concepts used to overturn accepted and constrained views: the fear of death and the immutability of form. The Taoists worked psychological metaphor long before Jung.

The oldest text on Taoist methods of *qi* cultivation is the *Neiye* (c.350 BCE) or *Inner Training*, with guided meditation, breath work and alignment (*zheng*), and the first references to the concepts that became fundamental to Taoist Internal Alchemy (*Neidan*): *Jing*, *Qi* and *Shen* (essence, energy and spirit).

The Taiqing (Great Clarity) tradition originated around the 3rd Century CE. The texts came into Ge Hong's possession, who summarised them in his *Baqu Zi* (*Book of the Master who Embraces Spontaneous Nature*). In Neidan alchemy, a central text is the *Cantong Qi* (*Seal of the Unity of the Three*), traditionally attributed to Wei Boyang.

Baldrian-Hussein has investigated the origins of the term *neidan* (see bibliography) and traced it to texts such as the *Zhouyi canton qi* and the *Guwen longhu jing*, tentatively dating it to the 9th century CE. Certainly by the 12th century it was defined as a system and associated with breathing techniques.

From the *Tianyuan ruyao jing*: 'The body of him who desires to nurture the inner elixir is modelled on the cauldron, his essence and breath represent lead and mercury, and the trigrams Kan and Li, water and fire.' The body then can be charged with energy and corresponded to the universe.

Kan and Li, the hexagrams 29 and 30, are the ingredients of the elixir of life.

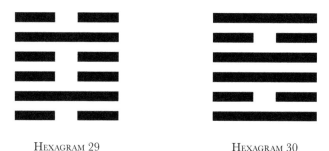

HEXAGRAM 29   HEXAGRAM 30

The diagrams of Yin and Yang and the Bagua or Eight Trigrams, along with the illustration of the Five Elements, are essential meditative sigils referenced in internal alchemical processes.

Observing the diagrams one can note a continual tension between opposites, but rather than resulting in stasis there is created a dynamism, a flow of movement. This is again reflective of the proposition that the requirement for progress is an active element of antithesis, which must be balanced even though the appearance may be antagonistic.

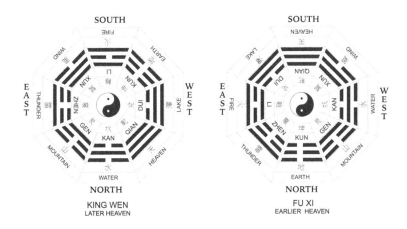

There are two Bagua, the Prenatal or Pre-Heaven design of Fu Xi, which demonstrates the polar nature of energy seeking to balance itself, and the Postnatal Bagua of King Wen denoting earthly transformation. The energies in this arrangement move clockwise around the periphery of the circle, beginning at *Zhen* (Thunder), signifying the awakening consciousness, and ending at *Gen* (Mountain), contemplation and completion.

Pure prenatal Yang or *Shen* energy transmutes to a Yin postnatal state at birth. A goal of Taoist alchemy is to regain the Yang Primordial (*Yuan*) energy and achieve a rebirth of consciousness.

In Taoist sorcery, the practitioner seeks contact with deities. In Internal Alchemy, the deities come to the practitioner. Specifics are petitioned for in ritual work; in Alchemy, the Tao supplies the needs of the practitioner holistically. There is 'Nothing to be done'. All will be revealed.

Although ritual and alchemy are two approaches to the same ultimate goal, and have methods and practices which overlap or complement one another (*Neigong*, inner work, is ritualistic in its own way), Internal Alchemy has certain advantages: it requires no equipment, and some of the exercises can be practiced almost anywhere. It is focused inwardly but prefers to be non-obsessive, despite seeing deities largely as involved in the inner landscape as opposed to entirely coming from 'out there'.

CORRESPONDENCE

Unifying diverse and otherwise unrelated items or agencies as meaningful correspondences is familiar as the Doctrine of Signatures and Tables of Correspondences in sympathetic magic. In the Doctrine of Signatures, for example, herbs resembling parts of the body would be used to treat problems with those parts. A foundation of Taoism is numerical significance, so anywhere that certain numbers occur suggests connectivity from one point to another, as we have noted. However, significance as soliptical obsession, where the individual becomes overwhelmed by a personally selective fatalism, seeing meaning in every synchronous event, is best avoided.

The *Wu Hsing* (*Wu Xing*) or 'Five Movers' represents phases or energies of transformation, rather than actual elements. A fundamental description of the course of nature, the process of duality is incorporated by having two cycles within it, the Creative (wood feeds fire, fire gives rise to earth, earth produces metal, metal forms water and water generates wood) and the Destructive (water quenches fire, fire melts metal, metal pierces wood, wood overcomes earth and earth absorbs water).

A host of correspondences were made to the Five Element system, including seasons, colours, numbers and the internal organs, which were accordingly paired: Wood related to the liver and gall bladder, Fire the heart and small intestine, Earth the stomach and spleen or pancreas, Metal the lungs and large intestine, and Water the kidneys and bladder. This list of associations was linked to the meridian theory of energetic channels as used in acupuncture and Qi Gong (energy work), part of what is known as Traditional Chinese Medicine (TCM); in fact TCM is an artificially produced compendium of representative Chinese therapies, compiled for political expediency. In reality the country has a vast range of different health theories and practices.

There are four elemental or Holy Creatures guiding the magician – The Green Dragon (Wood, the power of Imagination), White Tiger (Metal, Sensation), Red Phoenix (Fire, Intention) and Black Snake/Turtle (Water, Attention). These elemental powers have to be grounded on Earth, the Fifth Element, to be effective.

In the Five Element system, there is the idea of deities permeating the body and residing in the major internal organs (Lungs, Heart, Kidneys, Liver, Stomach). The *Wu-shih*, Five Corpses, are impure energies found within these five principal internal organs that must be eradicated by physical and meditative practice.

An independent school was formed on the *Wu Hsing* principle in the 4th and 3rd centuries BCE, which combined with the Yin-Yang *chia* (school) during the Han dynasty. Essence, sense, spirit, vitality and attention are the elements united in spiritual alchemy. Feminine Alchemy or Yin methodology requires adjustment in some practices because of the difference in physiology between male and female and the consideration of menstruation and the menopause.

Sun Bu-er, a 12th Century Immortal Sister, wrote poems on alchemical themes and practice, with lines such as:

'In the morning, greet the energy of the sun;
At night, inhale the vitality of the moon.'

Fixating on energy centres is in any case warned about as being potentially dangerous. The lower *dan tien* ('elixir field'), a point about three finger-widths below the navel, is particularly concentrated upon in martial arts. The other major energy centres are the middle heart point and the upper *dan t'ien* between the brows, the 'Third Eye'. Energy should be continuously flowing rather than static.

Inner Alchemical methods include breath work. There are many forms of breathing patterns. The In breath is the Yin breath; exhalation is classed as Yang. As Qi Gong, rhythmical breathing is combined with physical movement, typically based on balance and symmetry, like the familiar Cross-Crawl exercise, standing or lying, where the right elbow is touched to the left knee then vice versa, or, as still postures.

Nei Gong: Inner Work

'Darkness within darkness,
The gateway to all understanding.'
Lao Tzu.

On Reading The Alchemical Texts

THE TAOIST inner alchemical texts can't be quantified exactly. They are not 'science of transformation' manuals. Apart from deciphering their imagery as metaphorical and bearing in mind they are in translation, there is also the individual's interpretation on reading the texts as verse, even without poring over the commentaries.

The mind-body interface was not studied through empirical analysis in ancient China, although Taoism did offer treatment for mental conditions as an inchoate form of psychotherapy.

Hsing is the source of the mind and spiritual consciousness, *Ming* the origin of Qi, the breath of life: Nature and Life. Both arise from the prenatal void (*hsu*). Returning to the Void is a symbolic Inner Alchemy process of purifying the mind through the uniting of *K'an* and *Li*, water and fire or the energies of the kidneys and heart.

Preparatory to ritual, divination, and works of alchemy is the training of the mind, two of the most vital forces of which are the ability to *Concentrate* and to *Visualise*. There are various familiar Yogic exercises (Raja Yoga) for developing these capacities.

There are two general methods of Taoist Meditative Forms, which can be seen as Yin and Yang forms. *Tso-wang*, 'sitting and forgetting', is a meditation technique where the Taoist practitioner does not focus on an object but allows the mind to float freely, thereby partaking of *wu-wei*, non-action, and in this way becoming one with the Tao. *Ts'un-ssu*, 'maintaining thought', is by contrast the focus on a single object, in which is acquired the power of concentrated attention. This is the Fire (Yang) method, *Tso-wang* being the Water (Yin) method.

Another form of *Ts'un-ssu*, *Ts'un-shen* or 'maintaining deities', entails visualising the inner deities inhabiting the body.

Before engaging in either practice, the Taoist 'enters into the silence', *ju-ching*, by withdrawing to a quiet place and eliminating distractions.

A circle of light is imagined surrounding the body on three levels, for the physical, energetic and spiritual dimensions. A positive attitude of fearlessness is also cultivated. This is a method of 'Psychic Self Defence' that can be used in some social situations if feeling undermined by an individual or group. The physical position for Taoist meditation is often seated and relaxed rather than the usual cross-legged posture.

Most spiritual traditions recommend tranquillity as an ideal state to achieve. In Taoism the effort required to reach it is acknowledged, because it is not just a matter of finding calmness in a meditative session, but of maintaining that feeling throughout the day. On the Immortal Path, the Seven Emotions must be controlled. These are joy, happiness, love, anger, hatred, grief, and desire. Looking at the first three one might wonder why these should be felt to be injurious. I interpret the warning as against an excess of those emotions, such as hypersensitivity or sentimentality.

Regarding the current 'Mindfulness Movement', 'being in the present moment' isn't of itself enlightening, and doesn't have a moral or ethical dimension, as Roman Krznaric has pointed out (in *Carpe Diem Regained*). Taoist Meditation does not equate to this form.

IMAGES

Images (*xiang*) as cosmological emblems, and visualisations by adepts in meditation, are an intermediary between the substantive world and the Other. They form an important section in the I Ching.

The images of Demons are considered with great insight by Chun-yi Joyce Tsai in *Imagining the Supernatural Grotesque*, where she makes the point that lower social class psychology and prejudice could be projected onto images of demons along with fears of illness, physical imperfections and non-Chinese Otherness.

The use of mirrors as a protective device depends on their returning a view and exposing of the True Image of the demonic (meditation = reflection). Inner reflection deals with images arising and the seeking of the Original Form. A Ming manual cited in *Chinese Civilization: A Sourcebook* notes that demons cannot change their reflected forms in a mirror, and upon seeing their reflection would disappear without causing harm.

The word Mirror (*jing* or *jian*) is also used to indicate a model for applied principles in alchemical texts, such as the *Ruyao jing, Mirror for Compounding the Elixir*.

The incapacity to differentiate image from reality is portrayed in the tale of Zi Gao, Duke of She (6th century BCE), who was so enamoured of the image of dragons he had his home elaborately decorated with carvings of them. One day an actual one arrived, attracted by his obsession, and he ran off in terror, being unable to process a confrontation with the real thing.

The idea of the demonic world at a level juxtaposed to the concrete one, with attempts at order subject to human corruption as much as the intervention of demons, is conveyed in early Chinese fiction such as *Quelling the Demons' Revolt* (14th Century). It includes the classic motif of the 'Fairy Portrait', presented by a Taoist Immortal, with the figure in it escaping from the entrapment of imagery to become real; the character Eterna Hu is in turn heroic and demonic.

There is a vicariousness to our self-image-prompted vision of the world through a lens, never experiencing now, the moment, but recording it to be replayed again and again, pored over in examination of whether one is really 'There' – an uncertainty of being. This has occurred through the agency of photography and film, digital enhancement and all the enticements of virtual reality, the relativity of truth.

The progression from shadow plays to theatre, to the Victorian seance parlours and from there, a realised mass communication of disembodied voices via radio, to flickering images of the silver screen, was a shared experience; presently there is an isolating delivery of sound and vision.

At a time of simulation and dissimulation we might question whether we are becoming the shadows of our images. Our self-awareness is increasingly modified, if not even lessened by the images we create and receive in alternate space.

Image as haunting is portrayed by the Chinese spirit Hua Zhong Xian, bound to her captured image. Usually female, she is occasionally interpreted as taking possession of a painting, as noted previously. We never really see ourselves, only as reflection where our image is reversed. The photographic view, on the other hand, captures us the 'right way around'. We have become haunted without realising it. For the last couple of centuries we have been under the enchantment of our own idealised spectre, our eidolon.

How to face the Opponent: Break the Mirror.
'Les miroirs sont les portes par lesquelles la Mort va et vient.'
Jean Cocteau.

The 'Truth on Earth' chapter of the *Baopuzi* contains a technique for multiplying the body (*fenxing*), 'Bright Mirror', in order to communicate with deities and realise the tenfold aspects of the soul. In the 1993 biopic *Dragon: The Bruce Lee Story*, with Jason Scott Lee as Bruce, the Hall of Mirrors scene in *Enter the Dragon* is interwoven with a fantasy sequence of Lee fighting a demon.

'Remember,' says Lee's Shaolin master, 'the enemy has only images and illusions behind which he hides his true motives. Destroy the image and you will break the enemy.'

The Hall of Mirrors was also used in the Orson Welles film *The Lady from Shanghai* (1948). *Enter the Dragon's* director Robert Clouse was presumably familiar with the scene. Welles, a master illusionist, had his own demons to contend with.

A core aspect of Taoist ambition is to reveal the True Human, the Prenatal Self. This translates as the identity before the acquisition of false selves, the multiple personas adopted as we identify ourselves as our occupation, age, nationality, race, beliefs or non-beliefs. That is why Taoism is, in reality, unidentifiable, inexpressible. My words are a shadow-play in themselves.

The Actor has at least the rectitude, the honesty, that it is his or her profession. Constantly reaching to grasp the interface between our experiences of this world and the borderland of the Other, the mirror carried by the adept to reveal demons on his journey to the mountain is the one in which we find our own image.

As Baudrillard noted in *The Evil Demon of Images*, the mirror brings forth the Double, the 'diabolical seduction of images'. There is a second 'evil demon' he remarks upon in his essay, that of conformity. To be a non-conformist is to be outside of the norm, to rebel against regulation and the confines of sameness – breathing in another dimension.

Where the cult of celebrity is not a cult anymore but a feature of social engineering, alterity is selected for demonisation. Rebellion, acts of insurrection, have to be undertaken, because in a world where nothing is unrevealed and everywhere is present there will be a need to create a new soteriology.

TAO/IAO

To frame the resolution of East/West symbolically:
TAO = CROSS, PENTAGRAM AND MAGIC CIRCLE.

While 'Tao' is a relative translation and a fairly abstract construct as a word, as a symbol model it can be read to have significant components. TAO is then a primal and perfect designation for the elementary core of magic: The Cross of Duality; the Five Elements; and the Magic Circle.

Apart from the AO element, the name of the gods of rain and sea, the four dragon kings (Ao Ch'in, Ao Kuang, Ao Jun and Ao Shun), and which we can as well read as Alpha and Omega, TAO as an alphabet-symbolic representation of a Chinese transliteration has a value equivalent to the Gnostic IAO, an Archon pictured as 'serpent-faced' also used as a formula, each letter standing for a physical posture (like semaphore without the flags) with a corresponding energetic function. This is akin to Qi Gong exercises where holding a position activates energy channels in the meridians of the body.

Stand upright with the arms at the sides for I, extend arms and legs star-like for the A, and hold the arms in a circular position as if holding a ball in front of you for the O. To represent the TAO, the arms are obviously extended sideways in the first T form.

In Qi-energetic terms, when adopting the first position energy travels down the front of the body and up the spinal column; this is known as the Microcosmic Orbit (my teacher disliked this term, preferring the more traditional 'Small Circulation of Qi').

In the second posture, energy is extended through the arm and leg meridians, the Macrocosmic Orbit ('Large Circulation of Qi').

Finally, in the 'Holding the Ball' stance, (an example of *Zhang Zhuang*, or Standing Post Qi Gong), energy is extended into the earth and around the body.

The postures indicate the three primary theories and practices in Taoist internal alchemy. The cross is symbolic of being pinned to duality, Yin-Yang, between Heaven and Earth. The Pentagram symbolises the Five Elements in constant interaction, and the Circle is a magic sphere of both protection and invocation.

This is also an obvious basis for Western magic and religion.

So, the physical embodiment of a Gnostic Archon involves the meridian system – a cultural cross-dressing that possibly will not find favour amongst the purists in either Taoist or Gnostic scholarship.

THE MERIDIAN ENERGY MODEL

The 12 main meridians in Chinese traditional medicine are each named for an association with a particular organ: the Heart meridian, Lung meridian and so on.

Points located on the meridians are numbered thus for example; H1 for Heart meridian point 1, or L14, Lung meridian point 14. The eight extra meridians, the *Chi-jing ba-mai*, are referred to variously as Channels, or even Psychic Channels, Vessels or Reservoirs to differentiate them from the organ meridians. Homeostatic, Ancestral and Miraculous are other prefixes sometimes used, indicating the different aspects of their importance.

These act as storage mediums for Qi, and provide one of the

main frameworks for Qi Gong practice. They consist of the *Ren Mo* or Conceptual Vessel which runs in a straight line down the front of the body from the lower lip to the perineum, the *Du Mo* or Governing Vessel which runs from there up the back, over the top of the head and down to the upper palate, the *Chong Mo* or Thrusting Channel that runs through the centre of the body from base of trunk to top of head, the *Dai Mo*, Belt or Girdle Channel that encircles the waist, the *Yin* and *Yang Qiao* Vessels (*Qiao* means heel, a reference to the promotion of mobility), and the *Yin* and *Yang Wei* or Protective Vessels, connecting the meridians together and promoting balance.

The *luo*, collateral meridians, connect with the 365 points of the system, and are involved with the flow of nutritional and defensive Qi.

ENERGY POINTS ON THE REN AND DU CHANNELS

The *Yin Tang* point between the eyebrows is known as the upper *Dan Tien*, the Heavenly Pool or palate. By placing the tip of the tongue, which relates to the heart in TCM, to the roof of the mouth, the *Ren* and *Du* channels are connected in a circuit. *Ren* 17, in the midline between the nipples, can be massaged to release stress and emotional blocks or withheld feelings.

The middle *Dan Tien* relates to the solar plexus area. The lower *Dan Tien* is about three finger-widths below the navel, and can be thought of as a Qi storage area. The Sexual Centre is known by the delightful names of the Sperm Palace or (obviously in the case of women) the Ovarian Palace.

The Perineum, *Hui-Yin*, is called The Gate of Life and Death. The point beyond it, GV1, brings energies up the spinal column. The Sacrum is known as the Immortal Bone, possibly due to its 8 holes.

The *Ming-Men*, between the kidneys, translates as The Door of Life. The left kidney is Yin, the right Yang, and represent mother and father.

The centre opposite the heart, T-11, is an area of 'hot' energy.

C7, the large vertebra opposite the throat, is a junction for nerves of the hands and legs.

At the base of the skull, the Jade Pillow or God Mouth has a role in breath regulation and the promotion of Yin energy.

The *Bai Hui* or Meeting Place of a Thousand Spirits at the top of the head is in Taoist alchemical practice related to the North Pole and cosmologically to the North Star. It 'opens' to receive Heavenly Qi. Also it connects to the Pineal gland and mid-brain in the reception of knowledge.

THE THIRTEEN GHOST POINTS

The Thirteen Ghost Points (*Shi San Gui Xue*) are used as a Medical Qi Gong acupressure/acupuncture treatment for mental disorders; originally they were used for the treatment of demonic possession, where spirit 'infestations' were diagnosed and treated as if medical conditions.

They originate from acupuncturist and herbalist Sun Si-Miao in his *Prescriptions Worth a Thousand Gold Ducats* (*Beiji Qianjin Yaofang*, 652 CE). The points are ordered in Four Trinities plus one extra point. The recommendation is one session per Trinity.

Trinity 1:

Du 26 (Ghost Palace). Located above the upper lip midline. Connects to ancestral inheritance.

Lu 11 (Ghost Faith). Edge of thumb nail, radial side. Worldly affairs.

Sp 1 (Eye of Ghost). Medial side of big toe, posterior to nail. The Body.

Trinity 2:

Pc 7 (Ghost Heart). Middle of the wrist crease. Material desire.

Bl 62 (Ghost Path). Depression below the external malleolus. Dealing with the world.

Du 16 (Ghost Pillow). Back of neck, below the external occipital protuberance. Adaptation to change.

Trinity 3:

St 6 (Ghost Bed). At the angle of the jaw. Observing suffering.

Ren 24 (Ghost Market). At the centre of the groove below the lip. Appreciating one's resources.

Pc 8 (Ghost Cave). Centre of the palm. Self Acknowledgment.

Trinity 4:

Du 23 (Ghost Hall). Top of head on the midline. The ghost has taken over.
Ren 1 (Ghost Store). Centre of the perineum. Embracing the Self.

LI 11 (Ghost Official). Lateral end of transverse cubital crease on arm. Self-responsibility.

13th Point:

Gui Feng (Ghost Seal). Under the tongue. Assisting Enlightenment. Or, use Yin Tang, the Third Eye point.

The points were used in conjunction with the individual's 'inherent ghost point', which was determined by the year of birth; according to the 'Twelve Earthly Branches and Ten Heavenly Stems' chart, the counting system of the Chinese calendar that originated in the Shang dynasty c. 1250 BCE, different meridian points have a strong connection to the spirit realm each year.

Gui, apart from meaning ghost or demon, in terms of acupuncture for health can mean excess phlegm. This relates to the important place of the breath in Qi Gong. Respiration is the intermediary between the inner and outer worlds, and we have the term 'inspiration'. Asthma is a condition famously afflicting occultists, indicative esoterically of being between two worlds and struggling to adapt to this one from the rarefied air of the other; Crowley called his asthma 'the Storm Demon'.

Hand Forms to Exorcise Demonic Qi (Xie Qi)

The Chinese hand forms, equivalent to *mudras*, are employed to guide thought and energy just as energetic channelling can be initiated through the body's assumption of forms as in Tai Chi. In the model of the meridian system, the fingers and toes are initiating/terminating points for these subtle channels.

From thumb to little finger the associated meridians are in order: Lung, Large Intestine, Pericardium, *Sanjiao* and (two on the little finger) Heart and Small Intestine. (The *Sanjiao* or 'Triple Warmer' is a term in Traditional Chinese Medicine for a model of upper, middle and lower sections of the body related to various energetic functions. 'Warmer' or 'Heater' is slightly misleading, as the functions are related to more than just a notion of heat.)

'Energy' being a nebulous word, we can include 'psychic states' as patterns that are triggered by these forms. For example, there is a natural instinct to steeple the fingers together when deep in contemplation, or of holding the hands clasped in supplication or prayer. The exercise of the meridians is aimed at the eventual production of a purified simulacrum of the physical body, a spiritualised counterpart. This is inclusive of the Shadow. Therefore the method is one of 'sleight of hand': a conjuration of demons. Or, as in the case of the following, the exorcism of demons. (Another ancient shadow-play: casting silhouettes of the shapes made by the hands.)

Damo Mitchell in *A Comprehensive Guide to Daoist Nei Gong* translates *Xie Qi* as 'Demonic Qi', as illnesses were believed to originate in possession by demons or ghosts. The contemporary translation is usually 'Deviant Qi' and indicates energy that is blocked – not flowing as healthy, vital energy.

There is no particular term for the forms; I have come across *chuang-tai* used and also *shou yin*, but given the multiple meanings that a single Chinese term can hold, with up to five tonal values for each word, the latter can be translated in one sense as masturbation, which is not the sort of meditation we especially want to focus on here.

The power of a simple gesture is revealed in such a controversial subject as President Trump's delicate kinesics. The placement of forefinger and thumb tips together is either held to be a sign for 'OK' or in some cultures an insult. What may have originated as trolling converted the motion into a symbol for 'White Power', the connection of finger and thumb forming a 'P' shape while the other three fingers represented a 'W'. Whether trolling or not, it was soon taken up by far-right groups and signalling 'OK' was subverted into something definitely not 'OK'. In the operation of 'Black Magic', a contentious term, 'good' signs are reversed as a matter of course into 'evil' counterparts: the inversion of the cross, the misuse of the swastika, and so on. Not that I am suggesting Donald Trump is a black magician (although, see 'A Fascist Tulpa in the White House?', a review of Gary Lachman's *Dark Star Rising*). The swastika, incidentally, by now hopefully and most usually understood as having only been used in a corrupted form by the Nazis, is apart from its Buddhist association also a Taoist Immortal sign, and appears on the palms of the hands, soles of the feet and the forehead ('third eye' point) of the enlightened in its correct form, a clockwise rotating orientation,

The set included here is an 11 pattern version. The number equals 8 + 3; the eight *gua* or diagrams plus the three levels of power or being. 11 is also a representative number of ritual magic.

Here is a short description of the form (I've included an indication of which ones can be corresponded quite obviously to the IAO formula out of interest for students of gnostic mysticism. Naturally the distinction was not originally made by the Taoist alchemists.)

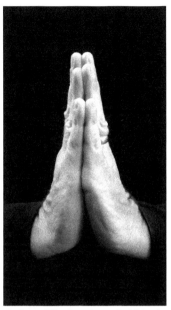

First position, *jingang hezhang*. The hands are held in the prayer or reverence position. I of IAO.

Sha position for healing, fingers locked and index fingers extended and held together.

The *Rin* or Strength position holds the hands together, fingers interlocked and middle fingers extended, the tips touching.

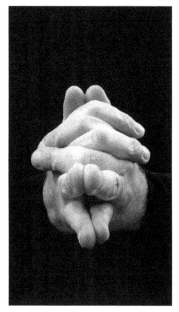

Tai, Harmony, again fingers locked with ring and little fingers extended and tips together.

Shen, directing energy, has the index fingers extended with middle fingers curled over them. This represents the caduceus or reptilian energy.

Kai, with all fingers interlocked, calms the mind and also admits premonitions.

Jen, the fingers are interlaced inwardly. This position signifies knowing others' thoughts.

Hua (a), palms forward, tips of thumbs and forefingers touch to form a triangle, the tattvic symbol for Fire. Hold this hand position and the following one in front of the forehead, connecting to the 'third eye' (*yin tang*) point between the brows. A of IAO.

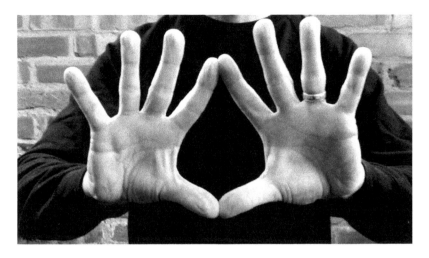

Hua (b), with the fingers spread, again tips of indexes and thumbs touching, is the mudra of harmony with nature, and so invisibility. Chuang-tzu's Butterfly.

Wu Chi, fingertips and thumbs touching to form a circle, as if holding a ball. Represents the Void. O of IAO.

Finally, right hand placed over left facing outward, thumb tips together, is the
position of *Tao*, enlightenment.

Because they are readily accessible, hand forms are ideal as an
introduction to Taoist alchemical work. They can be employed singly
or as a set.

Recommendations are to concentrate on the form, breathe
deeply and then note any resultant feelings or impressions that arise.

The above group of 11 can be linked smoothly together, one
form leading into another, to create a meditative and energetic ritual.

To be effective, the exercises are coordinated with the circulation
of *qi* through the psychic channels, and the extension of energy
around and beyond the body is visualised.

There are many other sets of hand forms, including one set where
the fingertips of the forefingers, middle and ring-fingers of both hands
are placed together or separated to represent the trigrams. Fingertips
connecting either singly or together with the thumb produce an
'energetic circuit' in esoteric traditions, with various effects upon the
body.

In the Tai Chi straight sword form, the free hand is formed into a
mudra, the forefinger and middle finger extended with the other two
fingers curled into the palm and the thumb folded over them. This is

called 'The Secret Sword Hand'. Popularly used in benediction, it can also be seen in the 'As above, so below' Hermetic symbolism (Number 23, the lower hand having three fingers extended), and in the sword form either merely represents an original intent of holding a dagger in that hand, or is used to direct energy. Some believe it is also used to strike Dim Mak points, but this may be debatable.

As exorcistic forms, the Demon Quelling Gesture (*qike yin*) is familiarly used at rock concerts: two middle fingers folded and held by the thumb, the forefinger and little finger extended. Warning (*weishe yin*) is another well-known form, with the forefinger extended.

Incidentally, some of the aggressive gestures associated with the old Eros/Thanatos conjunction, that is, sex and death, also act as 'Warding Off' forms: the V-sign, and the middle finger gesture.

War Demons

'Be extremely subtle, even to the point of formlessness. Be
extremely mysterious, even to the point of soundlessness.
Thereby you can be the director of the opponent's fate.'
The Art of War

Chiyou

The Art of War

THE ULTIMATE manifestation of the Shadow as the urge to annihilation
is warfare. We have seen that what is wrought in the aftermath of a
nuclear attack is the shadow of extinguished human life.

There is a little equivocation in my choice of title for this chapter.
Given the apocalyptic status of war, not much can be said of a Chinese
demonic attribution to it. China has a long history of internecine
struggles, conflict with invaders, and warfare; one of its eras is even
called 'The Warring States', yet war was not personified or perceived
as caused by a demon or demons. There are plague demons, famine
demons, flood demons and demons of death itself, but when it comes
to the grand orchestral cacophony of battle, they appear to be absent
from China's mythological cast-list. Only two supernatural beings
have any substantial formulation as associated with war – one of
those is a god, the other only partially a demon.

The Taoist war god Kuan-ti, Emperor Kuan, is actually intent upon peace, and is known as Fu-mo tu-ti, the Great Ruler who Banishes Demons in his role as exorcist. Originally a real person, General Kuan Yu, who was executed in 220 CE, he was admitted to the Taoist pantheon in the 16th century.

CHIYOU

Fernand Comte in *Dictionary of Mythology* described Tch'e-yeou as a demon, with a man's body, bull's feet, four eyes, six hands, a head of copper and with an iron forehead. But he is also known as a mythical king and ancestor of the Hmong people, a leader of the Nine Li tribe. His character is terrifying, fierce, shrewd, tyrannical and honoured. He therefore fluctuates between demon and war god, between the all-too human and a magical deity. At the battle of Zhuolo he faced the Yellow Emperor. Chiyou breathed out a fog, obscuring the light. Then he conjured up a storm. The Yellow Emperor responded by calling upon the demon Nuba to clear the clouds, and Chiyou was killed.

It might be wondered why such a tragic and devastating condition as warfare was not demonised. That it was a continual part of ancient Chinese life experience may have conditioned them to accept it fatalistically, but perhaps it was recognised that the conditions which could be subject to demonic interference were of nature, whereas war is man-made, so its causes and consequences are directly and undeniably human.

Stephen Mitchell has this as his interpretation of Lao Tzu, chapter 31:

'Man's enemies are not demons,
but human beings like himself.'

In other translations, demons are not mentioned. Richard Wilhelm has this:

'Whosoever would rejoice in the murder of men
cannot achieve his goal in the world.'

And Waley's translation has:

'And he who delights in the slaughter of men
Will never get what he looks for out of those who dwell
under heaven.'

Critics of Mitchell (see Stenudd) presume he uses demons in a figurative as opposed to literal sense, addressing the manner in which enemies are demonised. This may be; I don't know what Mitchell's intention was. Nevertheless, the lines are fine for our purposes when you interpret demons as independent non-human beings. What is then being expressed is one of the key sentiments of this book: the demonic is not necessarily The Adversary. It's important to make this distinction.

Mitchell's version may be artistically conceived, but in any case it conveys the thought that humans are found out to be far worse than demonic entities.

The great Taoist classic *The Art of War* (Sun-tzu ping-fa) was compiled during the Warring States period by a mysterious philosopher-general, Sun-tzu. A study of conflict and resolution, of acting according to situations and the profound realisation of the concept of Fullness and Emptiness, it is a mistake to believe it is purely a treatise on winning in combat when it is essentially about peace: 'Weapons are inauspicious instruments, not the tools of the enlightened.' By understanding conflict, it can be controlled. By realising the nature of the demonic, it can be brought into the service of the aware, rather than causing the unwary to serve demons.

Is the Tao humanistic? It is said in the *Tao Te Ching* that 'Heaven and earth are not human hearted. They regard myriad beings as straw dogs'. But this is an observation of the indifference of nature, not a reason to act without compassion. It says something of the manipulation of mass psychology, the clash of nations and tribes. *The Art of War* provides guidance on the cessation of opposition through a higher perspective, of regarding the psychology of the opponent and seeing different viewpoints from a higher ground (sometimes literally).

History is a blend of culture and warfare, and just as individually so for the world at large, before the demon can be absorbed darkness must be made visible. War is a negative but paradoxically compelling and driving force from which has been derived great advances in medicine, technology, communications and other aspects of endeavour.

The martial arts are alchemical when they are used for the transmutation of aggression. On the other hand the act of harming another human being, albeit in defence, is the point at which demons are summoned.

There is a confusion between aggression and violence. Aggression is not a negative quality when translated into, for example, attacking a problem. Aggressive action as force towards positive outcomes is not something to cower from. Here lies the differentiation between the 'good' and 'bad' demons: aggression versus transgression.

In terms of esoteric history and tradition, form and function, cultural transaction and synthesis, the magical and the martial worldviews have many points in common. Warfare is naturally inseparable from our experience of the world due to humanity's inherent state of primitive physical survival responses which can ideally be used creatively as the drive to achieve, separated from violence. The perception of the Other as that which must be conquered unfortunately becomes transferred via a mechanism of aberrant beliefs. At a base level we are obsessed by the Shadow as a mass categorisation, nationalism breeding antagonism toward the alien, the demonised refugee or outsider. Lack of empathy is also a consequence of obsession with self, which is perhaps and hopefully a passing phase on an evolutionary track.

As Magical Warfare was waged during the Second World War with groups led by such notaries as Dion Fortune concentrating their Will against Nazism, so at present we are wary of our freedoms being eroded in the course of Magical Terrorism, or the use of acts of terror to distract from what is happening as a political tactic (without becoming entangled in conspiracy-theorising).

Magic and Martial Arts have this connection, of being exotic, and of promising power to the sincere Seeker, intertwining like the snakes of the caduceus. Sometimes they run parallel to each other and sometimes they appear to overlap, as in the case of the search for that mysterious *elan vital*, the alchemists' elixir: Ch'i, the internal energy.

In the lore of the Middle East, the fallen angels and their offspring, the Nephilim, were responsible for teaching humans the killing points of the body, a secret knowledge passed down by demons. In China, acupuncture was developed when it was observed that arrow wounds sometimes had the unusual effect of seeming to cure certain other ailments affecting the victim. Therefore needles, first of bamboo and later of metal, were used to pierce the points outlined as having been affected by the arrows, but in a healing context. So too acupressure, whereby the fingertips alone were used for healing, or for killing as with the deadly art of Dim Mak, or meridian energy death point striking. This is studied in other culture's combative arts too, as for instance the Indian style of Kalarippayatu. Healing and killing are indubitably two sides of a coin.

The use of weapons has been posited as a factor in evolution, with the suggestion that man's discovery of weapons led to a better coordination of hand and eye, so developing the brain (Ardrey, Lorenz: see Fry, *War, Peace and Human Nature*).

Nature being indifferent to human comfort, it was felt to be a battle to survive. Some of the forces of the natural world appeared blatantly hostile. Magic evolved to aid humans in the quest for a better life, and as an outcome of the need for understanding existence and for taking charge. In our search for essential control over chaotic elements, magic sometimes shared with martial activity a leaning towards aggression as the way to power.

In ancient China, as in other cultures, during long periods of continual war, sorcery was combined with martial technique. Local militias used 'demon soldiers' as a part of their strategy (see Meulenbeld, 2015). The initiate in early Celestial Master communities received a register of *guibing lu* (demon soldiers) for occasions where they needed to be invoked against demons.

Charms and talismans were worn as means of protection, to add to a warrior's sense of invulnerability and to increase strength in battle. Swords and armour were reinforced with enchantments, and tactics were influenced by divination methods, such as the I Ching. Sorcerers, priests and astrologers advised generals and kings on battle strategy. Religious belief, which is belief in the unseen or occult, and militarism have had a longstanding relationship.

In ordinary life it is extremely rare that most people need a martial training. Is it therefore practised through fear of what might happen, or where the Form becomes a ritual of exorcism to deal with the projected Opponent? 'Shadow Boxing' then takes on a fuller interpretation of the name. 'Hell is other people' it has been said, where The Demonic is most definitely seen to take human form.

When religiosity is portrayed as a battlefield, a fight against evil or Spiritual Warfare, it is obvious we are imposing our own nature upon a plane that should surely be free of that distinction: the level of the trans-human. A combative approach is only self-defeating; as in the physical world, violence begets more violence. There is at least one Taoist Sorcerer I'm aware of who has been filmed brandishing a gun as an exorcism technique, as if demons are members of a street gang. This is just perpetuating a negative mind-set. We won't get anywhere by facing evil with that most predictable of human traits, the propensity to destructiveness. The corrosive world of base instincts only absorbs such energy and grows from it.

MAGICAL AND MARTIAL RITUAL

The methods of the discipline involved in traditional magic, either side of the Geopolitical Divide, are also the methods of martial arts. At the very foundation of both are breath control and relaxation. We also have the necessity of training the Will, or Intention, which involves visualisation practice, and the performance of Ritual, or in martial arts, the Form or Kata (pattern of techniques practiced in sequence), which embodies the content of the practitioner's intention. The Sifu or Master acts to initiate the student into arcane wisdom as does the High Priest or Adept.

The Chinese internal styles of martial art evolved from monasteries where the aim was the moral and ethical discipline of the monks; part of the training was cunningly effected through the physical work. The two melded together. So the idea of Yin and Yang, 'making the two one', found expression in the art of Tai Chi. Taoist martial arts are a perfect example of the integration of 'dark and light', exemplifying the principle of Yin/Yang. A major idea behind Taoist martial arts, and as portrayed in *The Art of War*, is avoidance of conflict, yet still winning the battle.

Martial Arts clubs operate similarly to magical orders. The student faces steady progression through a series of grades. Some styles of martial art even call their students disciples if they reach a certain level where they have a deep bond with the master, with the master presumably exhibiting an advanced level of adepthood. Such masters can be expected to be healers or to demonstrate psychic-type abilities, and to hold the secrets of life and death. In *The Power of Internal Martial Arts* B. K. Frantzis writes about his teacher's display of the ability to move him without physical contact, a phenomena similarly recorded for other sifus (p. 241).

There are a great variety of martial arts from different cultures with magical and spiritual elements, including Korokoro, a Nigerian ritual martial art intertwined with the Korokoro dance, Indonesian Silat within which you may find the use of talismans, Muay Thai, and so on. Some of them involve the conjuration of an inner force or demon as defensive or aggressive power. Such transformations are enshrined in the myth of the werewolf and other creatures.

Magic as it is *involved within* Martial Arts is not Magic *as* a martial art, which would include such exotic and entertaining applications as exploding sigils, curses and putting pins in wax dolls.

Footnote: Taoist Martial Arts

The commonly known Chinese internal arts are Tai Chi Chuan, Hsing I and Bagua. All three were linked together by Sun Lutang (1860-1933), a renowned master of *neijia* (internal) martial arts. They represent the three fundamental aspects of Taoist philosophy as I have indicated by the letters TAO, and they also have legendary founders, selected perhaps to give the styles an aura of mystery and kudos.

Tai Chi was supposedly created by the alchemist Chang San-feng (Zhang Sanfeng, 10th or 13th Century CE) when he observed a crane and a snake fighting, these two creatures representing Yin and Yang. This is the legendary origin which serves its purpose as allegory; the true historical roots of the art are still being debated. Tai Chi translates as 'Supreme Ultimate', the 'Chuan' part meaning fighting or fist.

The shamanic aspect of Tai Chi is its 'stalking energy', as noted by Larry Johnson (*Energetic Tai Chi Chuan*) – slow steps as if moving through a forest in the hunt for prey. Also the names of movements are a reference to animals, such as 'White Cranes Spreads Wings' and

'Snake Spits Venom'. The moves are not necessarily an emulation of the actual animal as they are an attempt to capture its essence. This referring to nature is a part of the two other arts as well.

Hsing I utilises the idea of the Five Elements, also being known as 'Five Element Boxing', and its founder according to tradition was General Yue Fei, a legendary 12th C. folk hero, who created it for his officers. (He also allegedly created the Eagle Claw style for his enlisted soldiers.) As the interpretation of Hsing I (*Xingyi*) is given as 'Mind-Form', or physical action led by Thought, the I or Yi of Intention is a very important aspect – the focus of True Will in order to achieve an objective. This is reflected in Hsing I's no-holds-barred ruthlessness in application.

Baguazhang, the martial art of the I Ching, we have already examined. The reputed founder (as is usual in such cases there is dispute over the origins) Dong Hai-chuan was said to be able to summon demons within himself to enhance his fighting ability.

Future Demonic

'For Every Demon there is a Master.' Chinese saying.

DIVERTED FROM their Old Ways, will there still be room in the neuromantic New World for demonic entities, and particular to this study, Demons of the Tao? Or, given their survival, how will Chinese demons differ in their evolution/devolution from their Western comrades? We have observed that these demons can be ambiguous creatures, flowing between good and bad, sometimes depending on the angle of viewing.

The shadow beings that are conscious aspects of the Taoist adept may continue to inform only up to that point where there still exists in the world the prospect of contrary values, of opposition and counterpart. Without these the world will be unrecognisable to human life. We may be moving towards such a condition, which will be inorganic life: the Artilect, a re-ordering of natural selection by machines – not necessarily a Terminator world, but something beyond our current comprehension. This, one could imagine as a possible but far-off future, although the pace of change has increased exponentially.

Taoist Sorcery is now being taught on the net. New information is channelled from realms of the Tao to enlightened adepts, and for a charge will graciously be disseminated among the populace, the 'ordinary people' (quote). A Chinese name will be provided for the neophyte, along with colourful robes for a further *nominal* fee.

Revelation rather than historical precedent is used to create Taoist cults around personalities, some of whom are curiously lacking in the requisite charisma.

Eastern 'magical initiation' at a fee has little to differentiate it from Western versions, it appears. In any case, I always liked the warning not to 'dabble' in the Occult. It was the only seemingly dangerous subject the word dabble was ever used in conjunction with apart from drugs. (Of course it enticed one to do the very thing warned against.)

We also find Taoist demonology transcribed to RPGs, and characterisations such as 'Taoverse'. The separation of mind from body and transference of individual consciousness into the computer dimension is, according to neuroscientists such as Michael Graziano, not only a possibility, but an inevitability, in which case the consciousness might find itself faced with the constructs of its own engineering, such as Taoist game-play demons. The gaming demons will be recognisably self-created yet still alarming to encounter. This is the point at which the term Virtual or Augmented Reality no longer acts as division, and becomes a crossing point into a continuous experience. We have yet to embrace the characteristics of Artificial Intelligence; based on its human creator as model, we could be confronted with dilemmas of emergent new life forms.

Everyone online essentially now practices a magical art, the use of the internet being synonymous with invocation/evocation, correspondence/connectivity (operations of sympathetic magic), the sublimation of power and the attainment of transcendence, journeying to the etheric /electronic planes (astral projection), conjuration or the achieving of instant gratification (wish fulfilment or results magic) and a new personal environment beyond the conditioned time/space framework (the ability to walk through walls).

Other magical attributions relating to the tech platforms include the Double as virtual version of the individual, Gesture technology, and haptive devices producing physical sensations with no immediately apparent connective physical causation, what would in previous times be thought the activity of disembodied spirits. (Schmidt, Cohen).

Our self-awareness as physical beings is increasingly modified, if not even lessened by the images we create in alternate space, and digitalised identities can be construed within the cyberworld as magical icons with quantifiable psyches constructed in electronic form. Along with this, our intent is directed in a new way, as the physical becomes relatively devalued. Progressing beyond the terms 'Virtual/Augmented/Mixed Reality' and even 'Real World', the digital environment informs our perception of reality, with activities becoming increasingly translated from the physical into this alternate realm. (See Ostrowicki).

An act of rebellion as a magical martial art is the re-establishing of embodiment, to reassert the physical, with some individuals coming offline after having found the electronic world still consisting of the negative aspects of the real.

Taoism is very body-focused. It works effects through physicality rather than intellection, even though it has a rich array of philosophical devices. To be separated from its primary medium of expression would entail a reassessment of its core values.

While some believe the apocalyptic threats of war, famine, plague and even death are being brought under control (a precarious claim: see Pinker's *The Better Angels of Our Nature*), we could speculate on whether demons are facing extinction – a final exorcism. What would the world be like without demons? We might have to re-invent them. The removal of the Shadow, and the consequent shadowless society of remedied psychopathies, would leave us bereft of some telling characteristics.

Certainly violence and cruelty would not be missed, but perhaps we might find too a lack of energy, as our world and its population became more uniform, regimented by peace. Without a resisting Opposite to engage us, without an inner opponent, our arts will surely become blandly controlled, if that is not already in the process of happening; China's State Administration for Radio, Film and Television (SARFT) has sought to ban supernatural themes, especially Taoist magic, although demons may be portrayed. (Radio Free Asia, June 2018).

The post-humanist condition is Inhumanism, the merging or submersion of ourselves with technology. This may also become a post-gender condition. A revived humanism will be a resistance to the Inhuman, to Artificial Life overwhelming us. It would have to rise beyond our present conformity to social norms, the grand narratives, the consensual hive-mind that has reduced the best of human attributes. The duality existing in the human world still exists in the machine, as binary code, so resistance is not, one hopes, futile.

I mentioned 'possession by technology' in the chapter 'The Unseen', with the old (as order or class) demonised. But this form of possession is not new. Global material advancement doesn't correspond to emotional or ethical development. To other life forms, the Human is demonic.

Capitalism as a prime element of humanism is paradoxically in opposition to the human, ultimately because it assumes a position of development for its own sake. Lyotard in *The Inhuman* has likened it to an entity, and the extension of its powers means parts of the human population are superfluous. We see this in action in controlled 'austerity' measures, the raising of the retirement age, the cut in pensions, in the diminishing of social security and help for the disabled and disadvantaged. The Chinese demon of capitalism is Taotie, the gluttonous devourer of people. And we must remember – originally, demons were invisible.

Time for an assault by Rebel Angels.

China's virtual equivalent of its Great Wall, intended to act as a partition against 'inharmonious information' (see Zhiyuan), is its Internet Great Firewall. Internal protest gave rise to the Grass Mud Horse (Caonima), a chimerical creation as a defiant magical meme along with other talismanic, homonymic creatures. (The phrase *'cao ni ma'* certainly does not mean Grass Mud Horse and is, as might be guessed, censored by the Chinese authorities.) A modern magical guerrilla campaign had been undertaken, with a grand scheme at its heart: liberation of the individual as free will. This sounds familiar.

These subversive chimeras are a magical act of rebelliousness no doubt demonic to the state attempting to suppress access to free information.

There is still a demonology but it tends to be interpreted in the language of the Information Society – as noise-related, of adverse signals, and interference in wave patterns: 'Demonology is not simply the study of demons, but of noise's assault on signal – a media theory *avant le lettre*' (Thacker, 2011).

We may be facing after all the most pernicious demon; the demon of ennui. It won't kill us, but it will drive us insane. In a world of similitude, of the undistinguished and indistinguishable, the new demons that arise will be working more subtly than the old ones.

The reactive pole to exclusivity is the 'relative truth' of the sanctity of individual viewpoints. Where this comes astray is for example in the 'free interpretation' of symbolism. It doesn't need expressing that there are around 7 billion experiences of the world. However, some things need universal delineation and definition, such as a Highway Code 'Stop' sign. Symbols derive their power from a clear and definite significance, and tampering with that dilutes their energy and effectiveness. Magic 101: Symbols have Meaning.

Mythic/magic symbolism is particularly vulnerably to being misappropriated, and not only by white supremacists. It is vital to guard against any encroachment upon the traditional interpretations of myth. Reinterpretation or elaboration as imaginative retelling while keeping the original basis intact is different from manipulation and deliberate alteration, or from effecting updates without appreciating what is already relevant content. From the viewpoint of seeing the demonic as myth, it must be protected because of its functional role in story-telling, the imaging and the release of imagination. Taoist demons have a definite integrative, evolutionary and evolving status, closing or crossing gaps of division; this is evident in their presence in magic, psychotherapy and alchemical motifs. So while new tech-led mythologies are being created, and China will certainly have a leading role in this, it's necessary to preserve the mythic and magical and to learn from its already loaded message.

Having now travelled from East to West and explored ever so slightly our thematic continuities and correspondences, we return as ever to that inner space, the involution of dark contemplation, the element of Yin. The Yin-side, the Gate, the Mysterious Feminine is where we find our capability to empathise – the quality of living the Other's life. Not to demonise, but to discern where and what the real demons are. Fragile as this capability is, and attacked by recurring extremist waves against it – the inevitability of reaction – we should hope that 'technological enhancement', an untrustworthy phrase, does not entirely overcome it.

THE *I CHING* (*Yi Jing* in the Pinyin method of translation) translates as *Book* or *Classic of Changes*.

Dated to the 2nd millennium BCE, texts have been discovered written on slips of bamboo. The standard text originates from Fei Zhi (c.50 BCE – 10 CE). It happily survived the book-burning instigated by the Legalists due to falling into a category that was exempt from destruction, although it has also been posited that it was kept safe by the peasant class.

The earliest copy has been found in the form of silk manuscripts in a lacquer box found during the Mawangdui tomb excavation in Changshu, Hunan in December 1973. The tomb dates to 168 BCE.

The mythic origin is that Fu Xi, an early (4th millennium BCE) legendary ruler of China, discovered the trigrams when he saw a 'dragon horse' emerging from the Yellow River with strange markings. This inspired him to compose the Ho Tu or Yellow River map, the initial plan of the *I Ching*. The combination of dragon and horse may be symbolic of the Yin/Yang dualism, with dragons representing the Heavenly, Fire aspect of Yang and horses the Earth, Yin.

About a thousand years later Emperor Yu had a similar strange encounter, this time with a tortoise climbing out of the Lo river with designs on its shell. This influenced the combining of the trigrams to form hexagrams. In reality it was probably the work of court scholars. King Wen, at the end of the Shang dynasty, formulated an interpretation or 'Judgement' of each of the hexagrams. Each line in each hexagram was given a meaning during the Zhou dynasty, so that by this time the entire context of the *I Ching* was comprehended.

Philosophically it then began to influence government, such as in the civil service. Confucius wrote commentaries on the *I Ching*, the *Shi Yi*, which were very influential. (Hua Ching Ni has stated that the Taoist study of the *I Ching* began much earlier than the Confucian, and is less rigid, with Confucius being guided by his ideals of an orderly world and society). Much later both Chiang Kai-shek and Mao Tse-tung consulted it in planning their campaigns, and to this day it is still regularly used both in the East and West as a method of decision making and a medium of counselling.

With modern archaeological discoveries it is now believed to be a synthesis of divinatory ideas from the Zhou era rather than the work of one figure.

APPENDIX II

THE EIGHT TRIGRAMS

		Energy Body	Quality	Meridian
Ch'ien	Heaven	Physical	Creative	Du
K'un	Earth	Qi	Receptive	Ren
Li	Fire	Psychic	Spiralling & Coiling	Dai
Kan	Water	Casual	Wave Energy	Yang Wei
Sun	Wind	Emotional	Amorphous	Yin Wei
Ken	Mountain	Individuality	Stillness & Light	Yin Chiao
Chen	Thunder	Thinking	Sudden Shock	Chong
Tui	Lake/Cloud	Tao	Formlessness	Yang Chiao

	Animal Forms	Body Areas
Ch'ien	Lion	Head
K'un	Unicorn	Stomach, Legs
Li	Hawk	Chest, Heart
Kan	Snake	Abdomen, Kidneys
Sun	Phoenix	Large intestine, Feet
Ken	Bear	Back
Chen	Dragon	Hios, Liver
Tui	Monkey	Shoulders, Lungs

THE FIVE ELEMENTS

Element	Organ	Season	Colour
Wood	Liver/Gall bladder	Spring	Green
Fire	Heart/Small intestine	Summer	Red
Earth	Stomach/Spleen	Late Summer	Yellow
Metal	Lungs/Large intestine	Autumn	White
Water	Kidneys/Bladder	Winter	Black/Blue

	Emotions (Yang/Yin)	Senses	Directions
Wood	Anger/Kindness	Eyes	East
Fire	Hate/Joy	Tongue	South
Earth	Worry/Openness	Mouth	Middle
Metal	Sadness/Courage	Nose	West
Water	Fear/Gentleness	Ears	North

When practicing walking exercises, stepping can be correlated to the Five Element model and affect the corresponding energy system:

Wood	Retreat
Fire	Step Right
Earth	Central Equilibrium
Metal	Advance
Water	Step Left

TIMES OF PEAK ENERGY FLOW THROUGH THE MERIDIANS

Lung	3:00–5:00 a.m.
Large Intestine	5:00–7:00 a.m.
Stomach	7:00–9:00 a.m.
Spleen	9:00–11:00 a.m.
Heart	11:00 a.m.–1:00 p.m.
Small Intestine	1:00–3:00 p.m.
Bladder	3:00–5:00 p.m.
Kidney	5:00–7:00 p.m.
Pericardium	7:00–9:00 p.m.
Sanjiao	9:00–11:00 p.m.
Gall Bladder	11:00 p.m.–1:00 a.m.
Liver	1:00–3:00 a.m.

THE CIRCULATORY FLOW OF QI

Earth to Heaven Yin Energy: Flows up the front of the legs and down the outside of the arms, and up the spine.

Heaven to Earth Yang Energy: Flows down the front of the body, up the inside of the arms and down the backs of the legs.

Appendix III

As is most commonly said, 'The Tao that can be named is not the true Tao', that is, tying the Tao to a label immediately limits it; so by extension 'The Taoist who can be named is not a true Taoist', most particularly those proclaiming themselves as one. Adopting a Chinese name, wearing robes and learning Chinese, however fluently, doesn't mean occupying a spirituality any more than other faiths' decorations and appurtenances. It is more a case of what you do than what you want to appear to be.

All respect to serious researchers. There are not so many of them as in other fields of study, but my list is not exhaustive, merely those I have most usually come across in my own studies.

Blofeld, John (1913-1987). British writer on Asian religion and philosophy, particularly Taoism and Buddhism.

Capra, Fritjof (b. 1939). Physicist, systems theorist, deep ecologist and educator, *The Tao of Physics: An Exploration of the Parallels Between Modern Physics and Eastern Mysticism* was first published in 1975 and continues to gain relevance with new discoveries in physics.

Cheng Man-ch'ing (1902-1975). Developed a short 37 movement Tai Chi form based on the Yang style long form. Moved to the US in 1964 and became one of the earliest teachers of Tai Chi in the west, particularly notable for his openness in teaching non-Chinese pupils.

Chia, Mantak (b. 1944). Popular author and teacher of Taoist Qi Gong.

Cleary, Thomas (b.1949). Has translated Sun-tzu's *The Art of War* and the commentaries of 18th century sage Liu Yiming. I particularly recommend *Immortal Sisters: Secret Teachings of Taoist Women*; the feminine element in Taoism as religion is in stark contrast to the major dogmatic male-dominated faiths, or at least how they have come to be interpreted by men over the ages. Cleary has stated that he prefers not to be restricted by monastic-style academia: 'There is too much oppression in a university setting' and 'I want to stay independent'.

Crowley, Aleister (1875-1947). It's impossible to avoid Crowley. Childish, cruel and vindictive personality as he was, he explored extensively both inwardly and outwardly and synthesised magical and philosophical thought from a variety of cultures. He had a respect for Taoism, working on the I Ching (see *Liber 27*).

Despeux, Catherine (b. 1945/6). French sinologist known for her work on Taoism and Tai Chi Chuan.

Fischer-Schreiber, Ingrid (b. 1956). A sinologist and freelance translator.

Guenon, Rene (1886-1951). Metaphysician and writer of the Traditionalist School. His studies in symbolism include work on Taoist themes.

Hoff, Benjamin (b. 1946). Author of *The Tao of Pooh* and *The Te of Piglet*. His books' popular appeal is valuable (at least to introduce children to Taoism) if controversial.

Huang, Chungliang 'Al' (b. 1930s). A friend of Alan Watts, Huang was involved in the West Coast human potential movement. Influential in popularising Tai Chi with his book *Embrace Tiger, Return to Mountain* (1973), his improvisational work mixed Tai Chi with dance movements. 'Tao without the ism' is a saying attributed to him.

Jung, C.G. (1875-1961). From 1915 to 1920 Jung studied Taoist and Indian thought while researching *Psychological Types*. In *Taoism and Jung: Synchronicity and the Self*, Harold Coward argues that Taoism was a greater influence on Jung than Hinduism, with the concept of Synchronicity depending on Jung's familiarity with the I Ching. Jung provided a foreword and commentary to Richard Wilhelm's translation of the *T'ai I Chin Hua Tsung Chih, or Secret of the Golden Flower*, along with the *Hui Ming Ching, the Book of Consciousness and Life*.

Kircher, Athanasius (1602-1680). German Jesuit scholar. Kircher had not visited China but compiled the reports of missionaries in *China Illustrata* (1667), a work that influenced and inspired the beginnings of Western sinology.

Kohn, Livia (b. 1956). A leading scholar of Taoism, author and editor of over 25 books.

Lagerwey, John (b.1946). Professor of Taoist history, author.

Lee, Bruce (Lee Jun Fan) (1940-1973). Also known as Siu-lung, 'Little Dragon'. Charismatic actor who introduced Kung Fu movies to the West and so incidentally helped to popularize not only Chinese martial arts but also its philosophy. Author of *The Tao of Jeet Kune Do*, his own syncretic fighting system.

Legge, James (1815-1897). Scottish sinologist and missionary, translated Chinese classics including the *I Ching* and *Tao Te Ching*.

Liebniz, Gottfried Wilhelm (1646-1716). Possibly the first major European philosopher to be interested in Chinese thought and to see Taoism in a sympathetic light as part of a singular truth and metaphysical language.

Luk, Charles (L'u Kuan Yu) (1898-1978). His book *Taoist Yoga: Alchemy and Immortality* (1970) is much referred to.

Maspero, Henri (1883-1945). Pioneer of Taoist studies. Died in Buchenwald concentration camp.

Merton, Thomas (1915-1968). A Catalan Trappist monk, Merton was keen on interfaith understanding and wrote over 70 books including *Thoughts on the East* and *The Way of Chuang Tzu*. He was found dead in his room after giving a talk at a conference, lying on his back with a short-circuited floor fan across his body. There was no autopsy and a wound was noticed in the back of his head. Curiously there is a theory he was murdered by the CIA. (See Hugh Turley and David Martin.)

Needham, Joseph (1900-1995). Sinologist, biochemist and historian, Needham proposed the *Science and Civilisation in China* project to Cambridge University Press in 1948, the first volume being published in 1954. It is still proceeding under the Needham Research Institute.

Pregadio, Fabrizio (b. 1957). Sinologist and translator of Taoist texts.

Robinet, Isabelle (1932-2000). Exceptional scholar and author concerned with the unity of Taoist thought and religion.

Saso, Michael (b.1930). An initiated Taoist priest of the Zhengyi school and author of *Taoism and the Rite of Cosmic Renewal* (1972) amongst other studies.

Schafer, Edward H. (1913-1991). American Sinologist, expert on the Tang Dynasty.

Schipper, Kristofer (b. 1934). In 1968 he became the first Westerner to be ordained as a Taoist priest in a verifiable line of transmission from Chang Tao-ling. Wrote *The Taoist Body*.

Seidel, Anna (1938-1991). German Sinologist and authority on Taoism.

Stein, Rolf A. (1911-1999). German born French Sinologist and Tibetologist.

Strickmann, Michel (1942-1994). Scholar of Taoism and Buddhism.

Verellen, Franciscus (b. 1952). Historian of Taoism.

Watts, Alan (1915-1973). A writer and philosopher, he published his first book, *The Spirit of Zen*, in 1936. A popularizer of Eastern philosophies, he became a US citizen in 1943. His last book was *Tao: The Watercourse Way*.

Richard Wilhelm (1873-1930). A Christian missionary who spent years in China and translated the *I* Ching and *The Secret of the Golden Flower*, a Taoist alchemical text. (Although this is the popular name, the Taiyi jinhua zongzhi actually means *Ancestral Teachings on the Golden Flower of Great Unity* (Pregadio). Lu Dongbin, the 'ancestor', revealed the work through spirit writing).

Wong, Eva (b.1951). Scholar, Qi Gong practitioner and author.

Needless to say there are others who some might feel should be included. Professor Terry Kleeman kindly advised me on the translation of *nuqing*. His book *Celestial Masters* has a chapter on 'Demons and the Dao'. Any further glaring omissions, mea culpa.

Appendix IV

Historical Figures

Chang Chueh. d. 184 CE. Founder of the Way of Supreme Peace Taoist school (*T'ai-p'ing tao*), which aimed at establishing equality and peace for all.

Chang Liang. d. 187 CE. An official during the Han dynasty and traditionally the founder of religious Taoism. Said to have achieved immortality by following *tao-yin* exercises and abstaining from eating grain.

Chang Po-tuan. 984-1082. Important representative of the School of the Inner Elixir in alchemy, author of the *Essay on the Awakening to the Truth* (*Wu-chen p'ien*).

Chang San-feng. c. 13th century Taoist alchemist and creator of Tai Chi Chuan.

Chang Tao-ling. c. 34-156. Credited with founding the Way of Celestial Masters sect (*'Five Pecks of Rice'* Taoism). Reformed religious practices.

Ch'en T'uan. c. 906-989. Taoist scholar and alchemist, said to be the creator of the diagram of primordial heaven (*hsien-t'ien-t'u*).

Chuang-tzu. c. 369-286 BCE. Author of the Taoist classic. Critic of Confucianism.

Dong Hai Chuan. 1797/1813-1882. Credited as the founder of the Baguazhang fighting style.

Fu Hsi. Mythic emperor, husband of Nu-kua, the female creator of mankind. Creator of music and the eight trigrams. Represented as having a snake's body.

Ge Hong or Ko Hung. 283-343. Author of the *Baopuzi* (*Pao p'u tzu*), 'He Who Holds to Simplicity'. The 20 Inner chapters (*neipian*) cover his alchemical studies. The second part, the 50 Outer chapters (*waipian*) stress ethics and reveal his early Confucian education.

Huang-Ti, the legendary Yellow Emperor. 2697-2597 or 2674-2575 BCE. The supposed author of the medical work the *Huang-ti Nei-ching*.

Hua T'o. 2nd to 3rd Century. Known as the creator of the Qi Gong set of exercises, the *'Five Animal Movements'*.

Hui Shih. c. 370-310 BCE. Friend of Chuang-tzu, a philosopher of the School of Names, which concerned itself with the relationship between names and reality.

Hui-tsung. 1082-1135. Sung emperor and supporter of Taoism. Encouraged the Tao-tsang's compilation.

K'ou Ch'ien-chih. 365-448. Reformer and organizer of Taoist ceremonies and rites.

Kiu Chang Chun. 1148-1227. Quanzhen Taoist, founder of the Dragon Gate sect.

K'ung-fu-tzu, K'ung-tzu or Confucius. 551-479 BCE. Wrote a number of works, his teachings are compiled in the *Analects*.

Lao-tzu, Lao Tan or Li Erh. 6th Century BCE traditional author of the *Tao Te Ching*.

Lieh-tzu. Warring States period philosopher, author of the work by his name.

Li Shao-chun. 2nd century BCE. Taoist sorcerer and alchemist.

Mo Ti. c. 468-376 BCE. Founder of Mohism, a philosophy of universal love.

Sun Bu'er. 1119-1182. Founded the *Purity and Tranquility* sect. Influential priestess and poet.

Sun Ssu-miao. 581-682. Taoist physician and scholar.

Sung Wen-ming. 6th century writer and reformer.

T'ao Hung-ching. 456-536. A follower of Ge Hong and the first to classify Taoist deities.

T'sou Yen. 3rd century BCE. Famous representative of the Yin-Yang School.

Wang Chongyang. 1113-1170. A founder of the Way of Complete Perfection (*Quanzhen*) Taoism.

Wang Pi. 226 – 249. Representative of neo-Taoism, commentator on the *Tao Te Ching* and *I Ching*.

Wei P'o-yang. 2nd century CE. Author of the oldest known alchemical treatise, *On the Uniting of Correspondences* (*Chou-i t'san-t'ung-chi*).

Wu-tsung. 814-846. T'ang emperor, a great supporter of Taoism to
the extent of suppressing Buddhism.

Yang Chu. 4ᵗʰ/3ʳᵈ century BCE philosopher. His teachings are in
the *Chuang-tzu* and other works; none of his own writings have
survived.

Yu Chi. d. 197 CE. Taoist scholar, miracle healer, and author of the
T'ai p'ing ch'ing-ling shu, *Book of Supreme Peace and Purity*, which gave
rise to the School of Supreme Peace (*t'ai-p'ing tao*).

Yang Hsiung. 53 BCEE to 18 CE. Tai Hsuan (*Great Mystery*) preacher.

Yu Yen. 1258-1314. Scholar, alchemist and interpreter of the I Ching.

Ba Gua – Eight Trigrams.

Bigu – The practice of not eating grain.

Chai – Rites of Purification in Ceremonial Taoism.

Chen-jen – The 'True Human'.

Chuan Chen Chia – The Complete Truth Taoist sect.

Chuan T'ien Tsun – Rotating in Worship of Heaven, a circle walking practice.

Da Chou Tien – 'Large circulation' of qi.

Diandao – Reversal, inversion. An important principle in inner alchemy.

Dan Tien – 'Elixir field', an energy centre of the body.

Dao shi – There are five general interpretations of the term *Dao shi*, according to the method of tonal pronunciation (four tones and a 'toneless' or neutral tone): mentor, Daoist priest, 'at that future time', to ram or compress earth, and 'contrary to expectation'. These interpretations are not so unconnected as they might at first appear.

Fang-shih – Magicians.

Fu jih-hsiang – 'Absorbing the image of the sun into oneself'. A perhaps complementary exercise to Hsuan-i (see below).

Gao shou – Mastery.

Hsiang sheng – Mutual arising.

Hsuan-i – Concentration on the Obscure One. Visualizing the sun and concentrating on the shadow it projects.

Jing – Essence.

Jing-shen – The spirit of vitality.

Ju-ching – To enter into the silence; primary stage before meditative work.

Ku-shen – Spirit of the Valley, supposedly identical with the Primordial Mother (Hsuan-p'in). The Valley is that empty place or Void to which flows water, and so a symbol of Tao.

Lao shi – Teacher.

Leifa – Thunder Rites. A tradition of Taoist sorcery that arose during the Song Dynasty and is still extant, consisting of using Fu sigils and charms, conjurations, trance work, shamanic journeying to other dimensions and exorcism.

Li – Ritual.

Lien-shu-ho-Tao – Cultivating the Void to merge with the Tao.

Lung-hu – Dragon and tiger, particularly in alchemy the Green Dragon and White Tiger, symbolizing Yang and Yin.

Lung-men – Dragon Gate. Apart from its association with a sect, the Dragon Gate separates the mortal and immortal realms.

Ming – Luminosity or enlightenment.

Ming Men – The gate of life.

Nei Gong – Inner Work.

Nei-shih / Nei-kunn – Inner Viewing.

Qi – Energy.

Qi Gong – Energy work, exercises.

San Bao – Three Treasures, Shen, Jing and Qi.

San Cai – Three Powers, Heaven, Earth and Human.

Shen – Spirit.

Shen-tung – Spiritual break through.

Shao Chou Tien – 'Small circulation' of qi.

Shou-i – 'Preserving the one', an inner alchemy meditative exercise. Deities within the body are visualized in order to unite with them, such as the Supreme One (T'ai-i).

Shun-liu – Going with the flow like water.

Song – Active relaxation.

Tao – The Way.

Tao-jia – Esoteric Taoism.

Tao Te Ching – The Classic of the Way and its Power.

Ts'o-ch'an – Mind control.

Ts'o-wang – 'Sitting and forgetting'.

Ts'un-shen – Maintaining Deities.

Ts'un-ssu – Maintaining thought.

Wei qi – Guardian Energy.

Wu – Non-being.

Wu-chi – Primordial formlessness.

Wu-ji-bi-fan – Things always reverse upon reaching an extreme.

Wu-wei – Non-action, or effortless action. Passive progress, alignment with nature.

Wu xing – Five Elements.

Xian – Enlightened person.

Xie Qi – Deviant or 'demonic' Qi.

Xin – The emotional mind.

Yi – Intent. Also, the 'Wisdom Mind'.

Yuan fen – Fateful coincidence.

Yuan Qi – Primordial or Prenatal Energy.

Zheng qi – Righteous qi. Balance of mind and body.

Ziran. Or, *Tzu-jan* – Being Oneself; Being Such of itself.

APPENDIX VI

THE DYNASTIES

Before 2070 BCE	Three Sovereigns and the Five Emperors
2070-1600 BCE	Xia Dynasty
1600-1046 BCE	Shang
1046-771 BCE	Western Zhou
770-256 BCE	Eastern Zhou
722-476 BCE	Divided into Spring and Autumn Period
475-221 BCE	And, the Warring States Period
221-206 BCE	Qin
206 BCE-9 CE	Western Han
9-23	Xin
25-220	Eastern Han
220-265	Three Kingdoms
265-317	Western Jin
317-420	Eastern Jin
420-589	Southern and Northern
581-618	Sui
618-907	Tang
907-960	Five Dynasties and Ten Kingdoms
960-1127	Northern Song
1127-1279	Southern Song
916-1125	Liao
1115-1234	Jin

1271-1368	Yuan
1368-1644	Ming
1644-1911	Qing
1912-Present	Republic of China (Taiwan)
1949-Present	People's Republic of China

As can be seen from the dates, there were overlaps in which dynasty was ruling or being overthrown.

BIBLIOGRAPHY

Alighieri, Dante, *The Divine Comedy: Inferno, Purgatorio, Paradiso*, trans. by Robin Kirkpatrick (Penguin Classics, 2012)

Anderson, Poul., *The Method of Holding the Three Ones: A Taoist Manual of Meditation of the Fourth Century AD* (London: Curzon, 1979)

Arendt, Hannah, *Eichmann in Jerusalem: A Report on the Banality of Evil* (Penguin, 1963)

Asma, Stephen T., (*On Monsters. An Unnatural History of Our Worst Fears,* (Oxford: Oxford University Press, 2009)

Bastian, Simon, *Qi Gong: Learning the Way* (Green Magic, 2013)

Bastian, Simon and David Cypher, *Kuan Yin in the West: Invocation and Evocation* (Hadean Press, 2014)

Baudrillard, Jean, *The Evil Demon of Images* (Sydney: Power Publications, 1987)

Berleant, Arnold, *The Aesthetics of Environment* (Philadelphia: Temple University Press, 1992)

Birrell, Anne, *Chinese Mythology: An Introduction* (The Johns Hopkins University Press, 1993)

Blofeld, John, *Secret and Sublime: Taoist Mysteries and Magic* (Allen & Unwin, 1973)

Boltz, Judith M., *A Survey of Taoist Literature, Tenth to Seventeenth Centuries* (University of California, 1987)

Boretz, Avron A., *Gods, Ghosts and Gangsters: Ritual Violence, Martial Arts and Masculinity on the Margins of Chinese Society (*Honolulu: University of Hawaii Press, 2011)

Brennan, J. H., *Experimental Magic* (Aquarian Press, 1972)

Breslow, Arieh Lev., *Beyond the Closed Door. Chinese Culture and the Creation of Tai Chi Ch'uan* (Almond Blossom Press, 1995)

Brondsted, Johannes, *The Vikings* (Penguin, 1960)

Buckley Ebrey, Patricia, ed., *Chinese Civilization: A Sourcebook* (Simon & Schuster, 1993)

Bulwer-Lytton, Edward, *Zanoni* (Forgotten Books, 2008)

Capra, Fritjof, *The Tao of Physics: An Exploration of the Parallels Between Modern Physics and Eastern Mysticism* (Shambhala, 1975)

Ch'eng-en, Wu, *Journey to the West*, trans. by W.J.F. Jenner (Foreign Languages Press, 1993)

Clarke, John James, *The Tao of the West: Western Transformations of Taoist Thought* (Routledge, 2000)

Cleary, Thomas, trans., *I Ching Mandalas: A Program of Study for the Book of Changes* (Shambhala Dragon Editions, 1989)

Cleary, Thomas, *Immortal Sisters: Secret Teachings of Taoist Women* (North Atlantic Books, 1996)

Cleary, Thomas, *Taoist Meditation: Methods for Cultivating a Healthy Mind and Body* (Shambhala, 2000)

Colegrave, Sukie, *The Spirit of the Valley: Androgyny and Chinese Thought* (Virago, 1979)

Cooper, J.C., *Taoism: The Way of the Mystic* (Aquarian Press, 1972)

Cordle, Daniel, *Postmodern Postures: Literature, Science and the Two Cultures Debate* (Routledge, 2017)

David-Neel, Alexandra, *Magic and Mystery in Tibet* (Souvenir Press, 2007)

Dean, Kenneth, *Taoist Ritual and Popular Cults of South-East China* (New Jersey: Princeton University Press, 1993)

Despeux, Catherine, *Taoism and Self-Knowledge*, (The Netherlands: Brill 2018)

Despeux, Catherine and Livia Kohn, *Women in Daoism* (Cambridge: Three Pines Press, 2003)

Diamond, Steven A., *Anger, Madness and the Daimonic: The Psychological Genesis of Violence, Evil and Creativity* (New York: State University of New York Press, 1999)

DuBose, Hampden C., *The Dragon, Image and Demon: or, The Three Religions of China – Confucianism, Buddhism and Taoism, giving an account of the Mythology, Idolatry and Demonolatry of the Chinese* (London: S.W. Partridge & Co., 1886)

Eagleton, Terry, *On Evil* (Yale University Press, 2011)

Ebrey, Patricia Buckley and Peter N. Gregory, eds., *Religion and Society in T'ang and Sung China* (University of Hawaii Press, 1993)

Fenton, Sasha, *Secrets of Chinese Divination: The Ancient Systems Revealed* (Sterling Publishing Co., 2003)

Fischer-Schreiber, Ingrid, *The Shambhala Dictionary of Taoism* (Boston: Shambhala, 1996)

Frantzis, Bruce Kumar, *The Power of Internal Martial Arts,* (North Atlantic Books, 1998)

Freud, Sigmund, *Totem and Taboo* (Routledge Classics, 2001)

Fritz, Robert, *The Path of Least Resistance* (Fawcett Columbine, 1989)

Fromm, Erich, *The Anatomy of Human Destructiveness* (Pimlico, 1997)

Fry, Douglas P., ed., *War, Peace and Human Nature: The Convergence of Evolutionary and Cultural Views* (Oxford: Oxford University Press, 2015)

Gibson, J.J., *The Ecological Approach to Visual Perception* (Boston: Houghton Mifflin, 1979)

Girardot, Norman J., *Myth and Meaning in Early Taoism: The Theme of Chaos (hun-tun)* (Berkeley: University of California, 1983)

Graziano, Michael, *Consciousness and the Social Brain* (Oxford: Oxford University Press, 2015)

Graziano, Michael, *The Spaces Between Us: A Story of Neuroscience, Evolution, and Human Nature* (USA: Oxford University Press, 2018)

Hammer, Leon, *Dragon Rises, Red Bird Flies. Psychology and Chinese Medicine* (Crucible, 1990)

Happold, F.C., *Mysticism. A Study and an Anthology* (Penguin, 1963)

Harari, Yuval Noah, *Sapiens. A Brief History of Humankind* (Vintage, 2011)

Izutsu, Toshihiko, *Sufism and Taoism: A Comparative Study of Key Philosophical Concepts* (University of California Press, 1992)

James, William, *The Varieties of Religious Experience* (Fount, 1977)

Johnson, Larry, *Energetic Tai Chi Chuan* (White Elephant Monastery, 1989)

Kaku, Michio, *Parallel Worlds: The Science of Alternative Universes and Our Future in the Cosmos* (Penguin, 2006)

Kashiwa, Ivan, trans., *Spirit Tokens of the Ling Qi Jing* (New York, Weatherhill Inc., 1997)

Katz, Paul R., *Demon Hordes and Burning Boats: The Cult of Marshal Wen in Late Imperial Chekiang* (New York: The State University of New York, 1995)

Kleeman, Terry, *Celestial Masters: History and Ritual in Early Daoist Communities* (Cambridge, MA: Harvard East Asia Institute, 2016)

Krznaric, Roman, *Carpe Diem Regained: The Vanishing Art of Seizing the Day* (Unbound, 2018)

K'uan Yu, Lu, *Taoist Yoga: Alchemy and Immortality* (Weiser, 1991)

Kuhn, Philip A., *Soulstealers: The Chinese Sorcery Scare of 1768* (Harvard University Press, 1992)

Lagerwey, John, *Taoist Ritual in Chinese Society and History* (New York: Macmillan, 1987)

Le Guin, Ursula K., *Lao Tzu Tao Te Ching. A Book About The Way and The Power of The Way* (Shambhala, 1997)

Leary, Timothy, *Exo-Psychology: A Manual on the Use of the Human Nervous System According to the Instructions of the Manufacturers* (HardPress Publishing, 2013)

Lin, Te, *Understand Chinese Mythology: Teach Yourself* (Hodder & Stoughton, 2012)

Lorenz, Konrad, *On Aggression* (Methuen, 1966)

Luo, Guanzhong, *Quelling the Demons' Revolt: A Novel from Ming Chin,* trans. by Patrick Henan (Columbia University Press, 2017)

MacLean, Paul, *The Triune Brain in Evolution: Role in Paleocerebral Functions* (Springer, 1990)

Maspero, Henri, *Taoism and Chinese Religion*, trans. by Frank A. Kierman (Jr. Quirin Press, 2014)

McCraw, Benjamin W. and Robert Arp, eds., *Philosophical Approaches to Demonology* (Routledge, 2017)

McGrath, S.J., *The Dark Ground of Spirit – Schelling and the Unconscious* (Routledge, 2012)

McKenna, Terence, *Food of the Gods: The Search for the Original Tree of Knowledge: A Radical History of Plants, Drugs and Human Evolution* (Rider, 1999)

Meinert, Carmen, ed., *Nature, Environment and Culture in East Asia: The Challenge of Climate Change* (The Netherlands: Brill, 2013)

Meulenbeld, M.R.E., *Demonic Warfare: Daoism, Territorial Networks, and the History of a Ming Novel* (University of Hawaii Press, 2015)

Mitchell, Damo, *A Comprehensive Guide to Daoist Nei Gong* (Singing Dragon, 2018)

Mitchell, Stephen, trans., *Tao Te Ching* (Frances Lincoln, 2015)

Mollier, Christine, *Buddhism and Taoism Face to Face: Scripture, Ritual and Iconographic Exchange in Medieval China* (University of Hawaii Press, 2009)

Montaigue, Erle, *Dim-Mak: Death-Point Striking* (Paladin Press, 1993)

Mu, Wang and Fabrizio Pregadio, trans., *Foundations of Internal Alchemy: The Taoist Practice of Neidan* (Golden Elixir Press, 2011)

Muldoon, Sylvan and Hereward Carrington, *Projection of the Astral Body* (The Lost Library, 2010)

Nam, Park Bok and Dan Miller, *The Fundamentals of Pa Kua Chang Volumes I and II* (Unique Publications, 1999)

Needham, Joseph, *Science and Civilization in China* (Cambridge: Cambridge University Press/Needham Research Institute, 1954-present)

Neiman, Susan, *Evil in Modern Thought: An Alternative History of Philosophy* (Princeton University Press, 2015)

Nevius, John Livingstone, *Demon Possession and Allied Themes, Being an Inductive Study of Phenomena of our Own Times* (Chicago: F.H. Revell Co., 1895)

Nienhauser, William H., *T'ang Dynasty Tales: A Guided Reader*, Volume 2 (World Scientific Publishing Company, 2010)

Ni, Maoshing, trans., *The Yellow Emperor's Classic of Medicine* (Shambhala, 1995)

Nienhauser, William H., *The Indiana Companion to Traditional Chinese Literature*, Part 1 (Indiana University Press, 1986)

Olson, Stuart Alve, *The Jade Emperor's Mind Seal Classic* (Inner Traditions, 2003)

Partridge, Christopher, *The Re-Enchantment of the West, Vol. I & II: Alternative Spiritualities, Sacralization, Popular Culture and Occulture* (T & T Clark International, 2005/2006)

Peperzak, Adriaan Theodoor, *System and History in Philosophy: On the Unity of Thought & Time, Text & Explanation, Solitude & Dialogue, Rhetoric & Truth in the Practice of Philosophy and its History* (New York: The State University of New York Press, 1986)

Pinker, Steven, *The Better Angels of Our Nature: Why Violence has Declined* (Viking, 2011)

Plotinus, *The Enneads*, trans. by Stephen MacKenna (Larson Publications Classic Reprint Series, 1993)

Po-tuan, Chang, *Understanding Reality: A Taoist Alchemical Classic*, trans. by Thomas Cleary (University of Hawaii Press, 1988)

Pregadio, Fabrizio, *Great Clarity: Daoism and Alchemy in Early Medieval China* (Stanford University Press, 2006)

Pregadio, Fabrizio, *The Encyclopedia of Taoism* (Routledge, 2008)

Pregadio, Fabrizio, *The Way of the Golden Elixir. An Introduction to Taoist Alchemy* (Golden Elixir Press, 2012)

Pregadio, Fabrizio, trans., *Taoist Internal Alchemy: An Anthology of Neidan Texts* (Golden Elixir Press, 2019)

Robinet, Isabelle, *The World Upside Down: Essays on Taoist Internal Alchemy* (Golden Elixir Press, 2011)

Schipper, Kristofer, *The Taoist Body* (University of California Press, 1993)

Schmidt, Eric and Jared Cohen, *The New Digital Age* (John Murray, 2013)

Schonberger, Martin, *I Ching and the Genetic Code: The Hidden Key of Life* (Aurora, 1992)

Seneca, *Letters from a Stoic*, trans. by Robin Campbell (Penguin, 2004)

Sim, Stuart, *Lyotard and the Inhuman* (Icon Books, 2001)

Spence, Lewis, *An Encyclopaedia of Occultism: A Compendium of Information on the Occult Sciences, Occult Personalities, Psychic Science, Magic, Demonology, Spiritism and Mysticism* (Forgotten Books, 2017)

Sterckx, Roel, *Chinese Thought: From Confucius to Cook Ding* (Pelican, 2020)

Sterckx, Roel, *The Animal and the Demon in Early China* (New York: The State University of New York Press, 2002)

Storr, Anthony, *The Essential Jung: Selected Writings* (Fontana Press, 1998)

Strickmann, Michel, 'On the Alchemy of T'ao Hung-ching', in *Facets of Taoism: Essays in Chinese Religion*, ed. by Holmes Welch and Anna Seidel (Yale University Press, 1979), pp. 123 – 192

Svendsen, Lars, *A Philosophy of Evil* (Dalkey Archive Press, 2010)

Swan, Frank, ed., *The Universe Next Door* (New Scientist, 2017)

Tanizaki, Jun'ichiro, *In Praise of Shadows* (Vintage Classics, 2001)

Turley, Hugh and David Martin, *The Martyrdom of Thomas Merton: An Investigation* (McCabe, 2018)

Tzu, Sun., *The Art of War*, trans. by Thomas Cleary (Shambhala, 1988)

von Glahn, Richard, *The Sinister Way: The Divine and the Demonic in Chinese Religious Culture* (University of California Press, 2004)

Waley, Arthur, trans., *Tao Te Ching* (Wordsworth Editions, 1997)

Walter, Katya, *Tao of Chaos: DNA and the I Ching* (Element, 1996)

Wang, David Der-Wei, *The Monster That Is History. History, Violence and Fictional Writing in Twentieth-Century China* (University of California Press, 2004)

Ware, James R., trans., *Alchemy, Medicine and Religion in the China of AD 320: The Nei Pien of Ko Hung* (New York: Dover, 1966)

Watts, Alan, *Tao: The Watercourse Way* (Arkana, 1992)

Whitehead, Neil L. and Sverker Finnstrom, eds., *Virtual War and Magical Death: Technologies and Imaginaries for Terror and Killing* (Duke University Press, 2013)

Wilhelm, Richard and Cary F., trans., *I Ching or Book of Changes* (Arkana, 1989)

Wilhelm, Richard, trans., *Tao Te Ching* (Arkana, 1985)

Wilhelm, Richard, trans., *The Secret of the Golden Flower. A Chinese Book of Life* (Arkana, 1984)

Williams, Jay G., *Return to the Roots: Platonic Philosophy and the I Ching*, English Edition (Ching Feng, 1991)

Wilson, Colin, *A Criminal History of Mankind* (Grafton, 1985)

Wilson, Robert Anton, *Quantum Psychology: How Brain Software Programs You and Your World* (New Falcon Publications, 1992)

Woodroffe, Sir John, *The Serpent Power* (Ganesh & Co., 2003)

Yan, Johnson F., *DNA and the I Ching* (North Atlantic Books, 1993)

Young, D., W. Tseng, and L. Zhou, 'Daoist Philosophy: Application in Psychotherapy', in *Asian Culture and Psychotherapy: Implications for East and West*, ed. by W. Tseng, S.C. Chang and M. Nishizono (University of Hawaii Press, 2005), pp. 142-155

Yudelove, Eric Steven, *The Tao and the Tree of Life* (Llewellyn Publications, 1996)

Zhiyuan, Xu, *Paper Tiger: Inside the Real China* (Head of Zeus Ltd., 2017)

Zhou, Egret Lulu, 'Dongfang Bubai, Online Fandom, and the Gender Politics of a Legendary Queer Icon in Post-Mao China', in *Boys' Love, Cosplay, and Androgynous Idols: Queer Fan Cultures in Mainland China, Hong Kong and Taiwan*, ed. by Maud Lavin, Ling Yang and Jing Jamie Zhou (Hong Kong University Press, 2017)

ARTICLES, ESSAYS AND PAPERS

Anadi, 'Freeing the Mind from the Prison of Non-Duality', Anadi teaching (undated)

Anderson, Poul, 'The Practice of Bugang', *Cahiers d'Extreme-Asie*, ·5 (1989), 15-53

Baldrian-Hussein, Farzeen, 'Inner Alchemy: Notes on the Origin and Use of the Term *Neidan*', *Cahiers d'Extreme-Asie*, 5 (1989), 163-190

Beebe, J., 'Presentations on Shadow and Individuation in China, in Personality Type in Depth', International Conference of Analytical Psychology and Chinese Culture (1998)

Bonardel, Francoise, 'Alchemical Esotericism and the Hermeneutics of Culture', in *Modern Esoteric Spirituality*, ed. by Anton Faivre and Jacob Needleman (London: SCM Press Ltd., 1993), 71-100

Boretz, Avron A, 'Martial Gods and Magic Swords: Identity, Myth and Violence in Chinese Popular Religion', *The Journal of Popular Culture*, 29 (1995), 93-109

Campany, Rob, 'Demons, Gods and Pilgrims: The Demonology of the Hsi-yu Chi', *Chinese Literature: Essays, Articles, Reviews*, (CLEAR), 7.1-2 (1985), 95-115

Childs-Johnson, Elizabeth, 'The Ghost Head Mask and Metamorphic Shang Imagery', *Early China* 20 (1995) 79-92

Coward, Harold, 'Taoism and Jung: Synchronicity and the Self', *Philosophy East and West*, 46.4 (1996) 477-495

Dannaway, Frederick R., 'Yoked to Earth: A Treatise on Corpse-Demons and Bigu', *Delaware Tea Society* (2009)

De Rolley, 'Putting the Devil on the Map: Demonology and Cosmography in the Renaissance', in *Boundaries, Extents and Circulations: Space and Spatiality in Early Modern Philosophy, ed. by* K. Vermeir and J. Regier (Springer International Publishing, 2016), 179-207

Fang, Tony.,'Yin-Yang: A New Perspective on Culture', *Management and Organization Review*, 8.1 (2012), 25-50

Fernback, Jan, 'Internet Ritual: A Case Study of Computer-Mediated Neopagan Religious Meaning', in *Practicing Religion in the Age of the Media. Explorations in Media, Religion, and Culture,* ed. by Stewart M. Hoover and Lynn Schofield Clark (Columbia University Press, 2002)

Fleming, Tessa, 'The Presence and Power of the Cosmic Yin: An Analysis of Chinese Women in Taoism', *Footnotes*, 2 (2009), 62-71

Freiberg, J.W., 'The Dialectic of Confucianism and Taoism in ancient China', *Dialectical Anthropology* (1977)

Granet, Marcel, 'Remarques sur le Taoisme Ancien', *Asia Major* 2 (1925), 146-151

Harper, Donald, 'A Chinese Demonography of the Third Century BC', *Harvard Journal of Asiatic Studies* 45 (1985), 459-98

How the Demons of Dementia Possess and Damage Brain Cells (2010) Report on Ecole Polytechnique Federale de Lausanne Brain Mind Institute research <https://www.eurekalert.org/pub_releases/2010-03/epfd-htd030310.php>

Ji, L.-J., A. Lee, and T. Guo, 'The Thinking Styles of Chinese People', in *The Oxford Handbook of Chinese Psychology*, ed. by M.H. Bond (Hong Kong: Oxford University Press, 2010), 155-167

Karcher, Stephen, 'Making Spirits Bright: Divination and the Demonic Image', *Eranos* 61 (1992)

Karcher, Stephen, 'Which Way I Fly is Hell: Divination and the Shadow of the West', *Spring* 55 (1994), 80-96

Kirkland, Russell, 'Taoism of the Western Imagination and the Taoism of China: De-colonializing the Exotic Teachings of the East', Presentation at the University of Tennessee (1997)

Kleeman, Terry, 'Daoism in the Third Century, in Purposes, Means and Convictions in Daoism', in *A Berlin Symposium*, ed. by Florian C. Reiter (2007)

Klein, Thoralf, 'The Missionary as Devil: Anti-Missionary Demonology in China, 1860-1930', in *Europe as the Other. External Perspectives on European Christianity*, ed. by J. Becker and B. Stanley (Vandenhoeck & Ruprecht, 2013), 119-148

Kleinjans, Everett, 'I Ching – Book of Symbolic Communication', presented at the Fifth International Conference of Chinese Philosophy on The Revitalisation and Reconstruction of Chinese Philosophy (San Diego, 1987)

Knights, Jessica, 'The Demons of Dementia', *The Lancet*, 8.3 (2009), 232

Lai, Whalen, 'Symbolism of Evil in China: The K'ung-Chia Myth Analyzed', *History of Religions*, 23.4 (1984), 316-343

Levy, Paul, 'Are We Possessed?', *Awaken in the Dream* (2010)

Lu, Hua, 'P53 and MDM2: Their Yin-Yang Intimacy', *Journal of Molecular Cell Biology*, 9.1 (2017), 1-2

McCreery, John, 'Negotiating with Demons: The Uses of Magical Language', *American Ethnologist*, 22.1 (1995), 144-164

Morgan, Carole, 'T'ang Geomancy: The Wu-hsing (Five Names) Theory and Its Legacy', *T'ang Studies* 8.9 (1990-91), 45-76

Needham, Joseph, 'The Historical Development of Alchemy and Early Chemistry', *Science and Civilization in China*, 5.3 (1976), 1-262

Ooi, Samuel Hio-Kee, 'A Study of Strategic Level Spiritual Warfare from a Chinese Perspective', *Asian Journal of Pentecostal Studies* (2006), 143-161

Ostrowicki, Michal, 'The Metaphysics of Electronic Being, *Comparative Literature and Culture* , 12.3 (2010)

Partridge, Christopher, 'Alien Demonology: The Christian Roots of the Malevolent Extraterrestrial in UFO Religions and Abduction Spiritualities', *Religion* 34 (2004), 163-189

Reiter, C. Florian, ed., 'Exorcism in Religious Daoism: A Berlin Symposium', *Asien-und Afrika-Studien der Humboldt-Universitat zu Berlin*, 36 (2011), 89-104

Sivin, Nathan, 'Chinese Alchemy and the Manipulation of Time', *Isis*, 67.4 (1976) < https://doi.org/10.1086/351666>

Sivin, Nathan, 'On the Word 'Taoist' as a Source of Perplexity. With Special Reference to the Relation of Science and Religion in Traditional China', *History of Religions*, 17 (1978), 303-30

Stambler, Morris and Chester Pearlman, 'Supervision as Revelation of the Pattern: I Ching Comments on "The Open Door"', *Family Process: A Multidisciplinary Journal of Family Study Research and Treatment*, 13.3 (1974), 371-384

Stenudd, Stefan, 'Fake Lao Tzu Quote: Man's enemies are not demons, but human beings like himself' (2017) <http://www.taoistic.com>

Sun, Key, 'How to Overcome Without Fighting: An Introduction to the Taoist Approach to Conflict Resolution', *Journal of Theoretical and Philosophical Psychology*, 15.2 (1995)

Thacker, Eugene, 'Occultural Studies 3.0: Devil's Switchboard', *Mute Magazine* (2011)

Tortchinov, Evgueni A., 'The Doctrine of the 'Mysterious Female' in Taoism: A Transpersonalist View', *International Journal of Transpersonal Studies*, 15.1 (1996), 1-23

Transpontine, Neil, 'A Fascist Tulpa in the White House? Right-Wing "Meme Magic" and the Rise of Trump', *Datacide Magazine for Noise and Politics* (2019)

Tsai, Chun-yi Joyce, 'Imagining the Supernatural Grotesque: Paintings of Zhong Kui and Demons in the Late Southern Song (1127-1279) and Yuan (1271-1368) Dynasties' (doctoral thesis, Columbia University, 2015)

Van Oudtshoorn, Andre, 'Where Have All the Demons Gone?: The Role and Place of the Devil in the Gospel of John', *New Testament Society of Southern Africa*, 51.1 (2017)

Wasserman, Martin, 'Kleist's "On the Puppet Theater": Wisdom from a Taoist Perspective', *Journal of Comparative Literature and Aesthetics* (2003)

Wong, Paul, 'Depth Positive Psychology of Jung' (2012) < http://www.drpaulwong.com/the-depth-positive-psychology-of-carl-jung/>

Xueting, Christine Ni, 'The Long List of Chinese Ghosts and Ghouls', RADII (2017)

Zhang, Qiong, 'About Gods, Demons and Miracles: The Jesuit Discourse on the Supernatural in Late Ming China', *Early Science and Medicine*, 4.1 (1999), 1-36

Zhang, Y. and others, 'Chinese Taoist Cognitive Psychotherapy in the Treatment of Generalized Anxiety Disorder in Contemporary China', *Transcultural Psychiatry*, 39.1 (2002), 115-129

INDEX

D

E

O

Oracle Bone Script 14, 91

P

Pace of *Yu* 45, 85, 86
Pao p'u tzu 45, 108
paper dolls 70
peachwood 68, 82

Pinyin 13
Plato 37, 49, 92, 115
Portentous and Propitious Mutant Prodigies 45
possession 33, 38, 42, 46, 49, 60, 68, 88, 116, 118, 126, 130, 133,
        153
Prescriptions Worth a Thousand Gold Ducats 116, 130

puppets 27, 69, 80
  puppet theater 27, 187

Q

Qabalah 113
Qi 19, 33, 49, 57, 69, 80, 86, 89, 91, 100, 112, 118, 122, 123, 128,
        129, 130, 133
  deviant 69, 133
  large circulation 128
  primordial 32
  small circulation 128
Qi Gong 19, 57, 69, 106, 112, 121, 122, 128, 129, 130, 131
Qimen Dunjia system 40
Quelling the Demons' Revolt 125

R

R-complex 49
Recipes for 52 Ailments 45
Record of Nine Cauldrons 45
rice 24, 62, 69, 70, 82
ruyi. See sacred knot

S

T

CPSIA information can be obtained
at www.ICGtesting.com
Printed in the USA
BVHW050421250123
656982BV00010B/572